D0269715

Aberdeenshire

3147163

# unthink

# unthink

CHRIS PALEY

CORONET

First published in Great Britain in 2014 by Coronet
An imprint of Hodder & Stoughton
An Hachette UK company

1

Copyright © Chris Paley 2014

The right of Chris Paley to be identified
as the Author of the Work has been asserted by him in accordance
with the Copyright, Designs and Patents Act 1988.

A CIP catalogue record for this title is available from the British Library

Hardback ISBN 9781444779714
Ebook ISBN 9781444779721

Typeset by Palimpsest Book Production Limited, Falkirk, Stirlingshire
Printed and bound by CPI Group (UK) Ltd, Croydon CR0 4YY

Hodder & Stoughton policy is to use papers that are natural, renewable and
recyclable products and made from wood grown in sustainable forests. The logging
and manufacturing processes are expected to conform to the environmental
regulations of the country of origin.

Hodder & Stoughton Ltd
338 Euston Road
London NW1 3BH
www.hodder.co.uk

For my teachers and others I have learnt from.

# CONTENTS

# The mind knows not the reasons of the brain

Your life is dominated by your unconscious mind: by thoughts you're unaware of, movements you don't realise you're making, and behaviour you think is caused by something else. Words, colours, mannerisms and other cues which you may not notice, and certainly don't realise are affecting you, change the way that you think. The confidence you have in your ability to reason and to consciously choose what to do is caused by a series of illusions which scientists are now uncovering, and which will change the way we see ourselves more than Darwin or Copernicus's discoveries did.

I want to bash you over the head with these facts. These are not odd quirks that are only observable in the laboratory or in rare circumstances. In all the important things you do and think about, whether dating, making moral decisions, empathising with others or choosing politicians, you, quite literally, don't know what you're doing.

This doesn't mean our conscious minds are useless. I want to explain why we have consciousness and what it does: how it is formed and how to use it better. In this book, we'll develop a social theory of consciousness which explains why we're tricked into thinking more of what we do is conscious than it really is. We'll find that our conscious brains are one of humanity's greatest adaptations. Their foundation is a model of ourselves as other people model us. We are conscious not to understand ourselves or what we will do, but to understand other people and predict what they will do. Our conscious brains enable us to live more complicated social lives than any other creature, and are the reason that humans rule the world. The theory explains why we evolved processes in the brain that we *experience*. But before we can do this, I have to convince you that consciousness doesn't do what you imagine it does.

All the greatest scientific advances have involved finding out that the world doesn't work in the way we experience it working: the world isn't what we imagine it to be. But the science described in this book does something which is in a way more profound: it tells us that what we experience about experience is wrong.

In the first part of this book, we'll find that we don't do things for the reasons we expect. Morals aren't rational, memories aren't the truth and we aren't as independent as we think we are.

We are mistaken about why we do what we do, and the second part of the book explains why. Most of what we imagine we do consciously is in fact done by the unconscious. We can't choose to lift a finger consciously, let alone pick a partner or form a judgement.

But if all the important stuff is done unconsciously, why don't we notice? Why do we have the impression that we make conscious decisions all day long? The third part of the book shows how consciousness is formed: from the outside in. We think we know why we're doing things even when we don't because we construct plausible reasons for why we do what we do and believe these reasons came first. We form our conscious experience of why we are doing what we are doing, how we feel and how we must have reasoned from our actions, our expressions and what we say. Consciousness isn't internal, it's external.

The fourth part explains why we have such a consciousness. This is the part of the book that everything else is leading to. We form consciousness from the outside in because that is what other people have to do when they want to understand us. Our success in life is dependent on predicting what other people will do. But we are only any good at this to the extent that we can predict what they will predict we will do. We need to be able to see ourselves not as we really are but as other people perceive us to be.

This is what consciousness gives us. We have evolved a better way of predicting what other members of our species will do than any other animal. We model other people as having minds, and by working out what they are thinking from the expressions on their faces, what they say and do, and what we know they have seen or heard, we can guess what they will do and how they will respond to what we do. But they are doing the same with us. So to really fill in the blanks about what is in their minds, we need a model of ourselves that approximates the way they are modelling us. Humans with such a model would be better at predicting and manipulating other humans, and so at achieving what they wanted socially than humans without such a model.

For such a model of ourselves to be truly effective it has to be slightly different to the model we have of other people. For example, we have to predict what other people will infer about us *before* they have the chance to make their inferences if we are to have the chance to change what we do based on its advice. We have to know what they can see in us, even though we can't see our own face or be looking down at our body all the time. We have to be aware of things that they do not know but might find out through our actions. But mostly our model of ourselves should infer what we're thinking in the way that other people infer what we're thinking.

Consciousness isn't designed for understanding ourselves, it's for understanding other people. This might seem surprising, but it shouldn't be. The greatest difference between us and other animals isn't the complexity of our abstract thinking, it's the complexity of our social relationships. We communicate in far more sophisticated ways than any other animals. We have more opportunities – through talking (and writing) – to change what other people think and what they will do. The people whose behaviour we are trying to change have to work out why we are saying or doing what we are saying or doing, and what effect we expect it to have. In turn, we have to work out what they will infer. To get a job or a date we have to be good at this game, and that, I will argue, is why we have evolved a conscious model of ourselves.

The final part of the book looks at one of the consequences of having a conscious model of ourselves. It investigates the conflict between what we consciously want to do and what older, better developed parts of our brain are telling us to do. It shows why we find using willpower so difficult, and describes what we know about tipping the balance in favour of conscious thought: if that is what you want to do.

We seem to have a perfectly good guide to how we think: our own thoughts. To know ourselves better, it seems that we need a little quiet time and honest reflection. But, disconcertingly, the results of scientists' experiments lead us to very different conclusions from those we'd form sitting by the fire deep in introspection. Our thoughts turn out to be a very bad guide to what we're thinking.

By the end of this book, it is possible that your view of

yourself will remain unchanged. You might be confident that your mind is deeper and your conscious experience really tells you why you act the way you do. This is understandable. But I hope most readers will join me in a second group. Reluctantly, and with a great deal of discomfort, I have accepted that my mind is playing tricks on me. I'm not the person I thought I was, and I don't do things for the reasons I thought I did.

## PART ONE

Thought alone cannot tell us
what thought is for

We can only understand ourselves through experiments on other people.

The only technique that has ever been successful in explaining the world around us is experimentation. Scientists drop things, pass electricity through them, heat them up, magnetise them and shoot subatomic particles at them. They do the same thing again and again and then they do it again from a different starting point, at a different temperature or at a different time of day.

Humans are rather intricate objects, but we too can only be understood through experimentation. To understand the heart you have to cut one up. To understand our cells you dye them, bung them under a microscope, and insert things into them.

Our minds aren't exempt from the rule. Introspection is flawed. We can't tell why we do what we do by reflecting on what we're thinking. We can't even work out why we're thinking what we're thinking by reflecting on what we're thinking.

Only experiments can tell us why we are the way we are, why we think what we think and do what we do. We need scientists to prod people, flash subliminal messages at them, trick them, scare them and make them fall in love. Then we need them to do the same things to other people at a different temperature, in a different language, beside another bridge, on a different day of the week and wearing different clothes. If they don't, we'll never understand ourselves.[1]

> If somebody mimics you a lot, then they're naturally empathic, like you a lot, or have been reading this book.

We all instinctively mimic people. We pick up our friends' turns of phrases, and mirror the stance of those we're talking to. We don't do this deliberately. When I went to university, I had no idea that I was developing a new accent until I went back to see my parents during the vacation. They joked that I was trying to become upper class. By the end of the holidays I was back to using northern inflection, and by the next holiday I was talking posh again. In my first job, I often noticed that in a meeting everybody, including me, would have their arms folded. Later in the same meeting we'd all be leaning back on our chairs, and at another point all be leaning forward. It might have been that had I stayed and become more senior I'd have learnt the secret signal on which all BP employees switch their body position, but it is more likely that we were all copying each other's postures without realising we were doing so.

Even though our mimicking isn't deliberate, it's still socially important. John Bargh and Tanya Chartrand (then at New York University) investigated when and why we mirror each other automatically.[2] They invited volunteers to discuss photography with someone the subjects thought was another volunteer, but who was in fact an experimenter. The experimenter either rubbed his face repeatedly during the task or shook his foot. When the researchers watched videotapes of the volunteers, they found that those paired with the foot-shaking experimenter shook their

4

foot a lot, and those working with the face-rubbing experimenter rubbed their face far more. But when they interviewed the volunteers at the end of the experiment, none of them had noticed that the person they worked with had any peculiar mannerisms. They certainly hadn't copied the experimenter on purpose.

People who are naturally empathic (or at least answer questionnaires in a way that convinces psychologists that they're naturally empathic) automatically mimic more, and when we want to get on with someone we are likely to imitate them without realising that we are doing so. It makes sense for our unconscious minds to talk directly to each other. Because we don't know we're mimicking, our unconscious minds can have a sincere discussion about our intentions. If we knew what the signals were, we'd fake them, just as a salesman always has a firm grip and a ready smile.

Playing Simon Says as a child can help you get laid as an adult.

When experimenters subtly mimic volunteers (so subtly that participants don't realise that they're being mimicked), the volunteers are more likely to report that their interaction with the experimenter went smoothly and that they liked the experimenter than volunteers who hadn't been mimicked.

A French researcher wondered whether the same technique could help romance.[3] Before a speed-dating session he coached some of the women taking part. In some of the dates he asked them to unobtrusively mimic their potential partner's speech and body language. So if the man asked: 'You really do that?' they should reply: 'Yes, I really do that!' instead of just 'Yes.' If he scratched his ear, they should scratch their own a few seconds later.

At the end of the speed-dating session, the researchers gave forms to all participants asking them what they'd thought of the people they'd met and whether they'd like to meet any of them again. Professor Guéguen found that when the women copied the men they were rated as being sexier and more of the men requested a second date.

When you go on a date you might put thought into choosing the right restaurant, saying the right things and wearing the most flattering clothes. But it could be something you don't realise you're doing, and your date doesn't notice, that determines how well you get on.

Imitation is the sincerest form of flattery and the quickest way for a waitress to make a buck.

You might think you know why you give a particularly large tip to a waitress – whether it's the service, the food or her smile. But in a Dutch experiment,[4] waitresses who agreed to repeat orders back to customers (saying the Dutch equivalent of 'a hamburger and fries' instead of 'yes' or 'I got that') received a third more tips. Not only that, the average tip was nearly 70% larger. Interestingly, most waitresses don't know this and when they aren't told whether to mimic or not they slave the night away for a fraction of the money they could have been getting.

If it's not worrying enough that waitresses can be taught to reach into your wallet without you realising what they're doing, psychologists have shown that mimicking can improve the relationship we have with computers.[5] In their experiment, students listened to an avatar tell them about a plan to improve security on campus by making all students carry ID. When the avatar was programmed such that its head moved in exactly the same way as the listener's, but with a four-second delay (just long enough so that the mirroring wasn't noticeable), the students liked the avatar more, thought it more realistic, and even found its arguments more persuasive.

Imitation is a ubiquitous social lubricant, and you need to be on your guard for dates, waitresses and even computers copying what you do in order to change what you do.

We live through metaphors, and metaphors live through us: warm days make warm people.

Some metaphors are surprisingly consistent.[6] Ideas are often seen as edible, for example. Perhaps you are reading this book because you have a thirst for knowledge, or a voracious appetite for new thinking. You hope that you can sink your teeth into the meaty chapters and that I'm not just going to serve you some half-baked theories which you'll have trouble swallowing.

If ideas contain nourishment then, metaphorically speaking, people have a temperature. Somebody can be warm towards us, but then a chilly reception can leave us feeling cold. An icy demeanour, a frosty glare or a wintry smile all indicate a less than sunny disposition, while difficult relationships thaw as they improve. This metaphor isn't just an interesting literary oddity however; experiments show that it goes beyond words and impacts the way we perceive the world.

In one study,[7] undergraduates either recalled a situation in which they'd been excluded or one in which they'd been included. The experimenters then told the students that the lab mainte-nance staff wanted to know whether the temperature was all right. What did they think it was? Those who'd recalled the time that they'd been given the cold shoulder estimated that the temperature was nearly three degrees chillier. The same researchers also found that people who'd been ostracised in a group task were more likely to want warm food like coffee and soup afterwards than those who hadn't.

But can it work the other way? On sunny days are we more pleasant to each other? Possibly. In the lift to another experiment,[8] a researcher gave participants a cup of hot or iced coffee to look after while he took their name and details. Shortly afterwards, the participants received some information on an imaginary person and rated their personalities. Those who had held the hot coffee ranked the person as being warmer than those who'd looked after the cold cup. People who had held something warm were also significantly more likely to choose a gift for a friend rather than themselves as a reward for taking part: not only did they rank other people as being warmer, they became warmer themselves.

Smooth salesmen can always do with a little polish.

The warm vs. cold metaphor isn't the only one that affects the way we act. Sometimes relationships go smoothly, but they can be rougher with an abrasive, coarse partner. After people complete a simple puzzle covered in sandpaper they rate vignettes describing a social interaction as being less co-ordinated than those who'd completed the same puzzle with smooth pieces.[9] They also act more co-operatively among themselves, splitting a gift of lottery tickets more fairly with a partner.

The stereotype of a salesman is someone with slicked-back hair, a shiny suit and dazzling white teeth. These traits might make them better at their job of smoothly shifting whatever it is they are selling. But then again, would the stereotypical salesman split his lottery winnings with you?

Forget fashion fads; red makes everyone sexier.

As well as linking concepts through verbal metaphors, we also couple some activities with visual symbols. Romance, for example, is strongly associated with the colour red. Robert Burns wrote that his love was like a red, red rose, and on Valentine's Day there are few blue or green cards for sale. If Chris de Burgh had sung of the lady in black we'd have expected a song about death rather than attraction. Scarlet women operate in red-light districts, and even respectable ladies wear red lipstick when they want to seduce their husbands.

This red/romance link is just as effective at altering our attitudes as verbal metaphors are. In one experiment,[10] women assessed a series of pictures of men on different colour borders, and with different coloured clothing. On a 1–9 scale of attractiveness, men in red shirts or whose photos were placed in a red border gained an extra point.

If you think you'll always be alone it's more likely to happen.

Being single is bad for you, and expecting to remain single is bad for the people around you. Apart from the unpleasant feeling of being lonesome, it has health repercussions. Social isolation increases the mortality rate from cancer and cardiovascular disease, possibly because lonely people deal with stress less effectively.[11] The pain of living alone also increases the suicide rate.

You might therefore expect solitary people to be nicer to others in order to make friends, and to volunteer for charity in order to meet people. In fact, the opposite seems to be the case. Married people are more likely to give time to charity and even drive more considerately. But this correspondence could be caused by numerous factors. It might be that nice, caring people are more likely to find love and make a success of it. It could be that a third factor, such as religion, encourages people both to get married and to help others.

To find out whether the prospect of loneliness increased people's care for others or diminished it, researchers conducted a devious series of experiments.[12] They told students that they had designed a questionnaire that could accurately predict how likely they were to be alone. The students sat the test, and were given feedback. In fact, the psychologists couldn't tell anything from the survey about how likely people were to find happiness with others, though the questions were the sort of things you might expect in such a test, asking whether the respondent was talkative, moody, outgoing, dominant or submissive.

Nevertheless, the researchers told a random selection of the students that their answers showed they were likely to have a long and stable marriage and would probably always be around people who cared about them. They told others that they were the type who would end up alone in life. Perhaps these students would have friends now, they might even marry once or possibly several times, but the relationships were likely to be short-lived, and as they aged they would be alone more and more.

After the test, the psychologists gave the students the chance to be caring. In one experiment, they said that they were collecting for charity and left the students alone with the box. Those who thought they would be loved in the future gave nearly four times as much. In another, the students believed that they were about to do a second test, on creativity, but as the experimenter went to get the tests she knocked a cup of pencils on the floor. Two-thirds of those who believed that they would have close relationships in the future helped her pick them up, compared to only one in six of those who anticipated a future alone.[13]

## Never date a psychologist.

Scientists aren't most people's idea of a hot date. There are disappointingly few films in which the bespectacled, lab-coat-wearing geek gets the girl. But we now know that scientists have been busy improving their chances.

If you go on a date with a diligent psychologist you can expect them to be wearing red. They will take you to a restaurant where the heating is turned up too high and avoid a table near the door. The cutlery in the restaurant will have smooth handles. When you touch your ear, they will touch theirs. They will say remarkably similar things to you a few seconds after you have said them. You will finally be sure your prospective partner has done their homework when they suggest that you stay for coffee but skip the gelato. After all, they want a hot date.

None of these are reasons not to date a psychologist. The problem is that psychologists can't think of romance in the way that other people do. They can't accept love as a mystery, talk of fate with a straight face or dream of Cupid's arrow. Browse through your bookshelves or your music collection and the odds are that they are dominated by writers and musicians trying to describe what happens when a boy meets a girl. Scientists too are intrigued by the riddle. But scientists want answers, and they know how to get them.

We know that red makes people more attractive not because somebody sang about it but because somebody ran the tests.

We know that mimicking makes people sexier because somebody rigged a speed-dating session. The only way to find out what happens when a boy meets a girl is to introduce them, manipulate them and watch. So if you date a psychologist, you'll never be quite sure whether he or she's in love with you or simply experimenting on you.

Chemicals in the brain determine how trusting we are, but buying more of the chemical shows you're gullible enough already.

Researchers have an investment game which allows them to measure how trusting we are. In this game, participants are granted a sum of money. They can keep the cash and walk away, or they can give some of it to another participant playing the role of trustee. In the hands of the trustee, the money is always tripled. However, the trustee chooses whether to give any of the money (including the original principal) back to the investor or to keep it all himself. The decision whether to invest any money is therefore driven by whether or not you have any faith in the trustee.

The trustee in one version of the game is anonymous. Participants don't know who they're giving their money to, and the trustee doesn't know who he's receiving it from. Participants play the game only once with any partner. If players approach the game sensibly, it seems that they shouldn't give any of their money to the trustee. From the trustee's perspective, there's no reason he shouldn't take all of the money for himself. He's never going to meet the person he took the money from, and they won't know who he is anyway. The players who have the money to start with can reason in the same way as the trustee, and realising that he has no incentive not to run off with their cash, they should keep the principal for themselves.

But, thankfully, real people don't reason like this. In one experiment with twenty-nine participants, not one of them kept back all their money from the trustee. A fifth of the players placed all of their money with them. It was also a good risk: the average trustee gave back more money than they'd received, and both players were better off.

Trust is one of the magical, irrational ingredients that makes human relationships work – and now you can bottle it. Oxytocin facilitates lactation and childbirth in women, and helps regulate maternal behaviour. It is released at orgasm in both men and women. When volunteers receive a dose of the hormone before playing the investment game they give significantly more money to the trustees, and were more than twice as likely to trust all of their money to them as those who'd received a placebo.[14]

It's probably not a surprise that you can now buy oxytocin over the Internet. The makers of one product advise business people to spray it around their desk and conference room to gain an 'instant competitive edge', and promise that if you are a single man it will help you get women who are 'out of your league'. As potential dates and business partners have to trust you pretty thoroughly before they will snort something out of a bottle you give to them, the makers of the hormone provide it in a perfume-like spray to be applied to your clothes. The idea is that the hormone will waft undetected into the nostrils of those around.

But before you place your trust in the marketing it's worth remembering that anybody spraying oxytocin onto their shirt several times a day is receiving a far larger exposure to the chemical than those around them. So if you meet an extremely gullible person, there's a chance that they're wearing oxytocin – whether or not the spray works.

If you want to get on in politics, spending time in the gym and visiting plastic surgeons is as important as writing manifestos and canvassing voters.

Since the earliest democracies, there have been worries that the electorate isn't sure what it is doing when it casts its ballot. In *The Republic*, Plato argued that the best qualified people for political power (philosophers, obviously) were very rarely selected. He compared leaders to sailors who knew nothing of captaining a ship, claimed that it couldn't be taught, and gained control of the vessel by means that had nothing to do with their navigational ability or understanding of sailing.

Plato's worries inspired a study to find out whether children were as good, or bad, as adults at choosing leaders. Researchers asked six hundred Swiss children, aged between five and thirteen, to imagine that they were going on a voyage and to choose a captain for their boat.[15] The alternative 'captains' were in fact running against each other in the French parliamentary elections. The kids' preferred skippers won the real election seven times out of ten.

Perhaps this study shows that our political understanding develops early and we should lower the age of franchise. But what did the researchers learn about children's preferred policies? Did the children think that a candidate who would lower taxes was the best skipper because then their parents could give them more pocket money? Did the youngsters favour an increase in education spending or a reduction?

In fact, the researchers couldn't determine any of these things from their study. They didn't tell the children about the policies or navigational ability of the captains. All the children received to help them make their decision, and accurately predict the election, were photos of the possible captains.

## Remembering something doesn't mean it happened.

We come to the truth in many ways. We read books, think, listen to other people and experience things directly. Other people lie sometimes. They skip the important details. Our thoughts are sometimes mangled. The most convincing way to learn things is to experience them ourselves. Our memories seem to be our unmediated store of the truth: the things we know for certain happened. But other people can give us memories of things we never experienced.

Elizabeth Loftus and colleagues conducted one of the earliest experiments showing how to do this, and highlighting how dangerous it is to rely on what we remember.[16] They showed volunteers a clip of a road accident. Afterwards, they asked some of the participants, 'About how fast were the cars going when they smashed into each other?' They asked others how fast they were going when they *collided*, *bumped*, *contacted* or *hit*. Participants who heard the question with the verb *smashed* estimated that the cars were going faster.*

A week later, the experimenters contacted the participants again and asked them further questions on what they remembered about the accident. In particular, was there any broken glass at the scene? Those who'd been asked how fast the cars

---

*The verb *contacted* elicited the lowest estimates of speed. Worth remembering if you're ever responsible for a smash.

were going when they *smashed* were more than twice as likely to erroneously remember seeing broken glass after the accident. A single, apparently innocuous word changed what people remembered, and afterwards their memories assembled all the details of the accident in order to make it consistent.

This was an early experiment. Researchers have since become bolder and better at manipulating people's memories. They've had participants remember robbers carrying a screwdriver that wasn't there.[17] In controversial experiments, they've implanted memories of childhood events that never happened, including being lost in a shopping centre, taking a flight in a hot air balloon and even meeting Bugs Bunny (a Warner Brothers character) on a trip to Disneyland.[18]

When *The X-Files* was popular, the number of reported alien abductions, some recovered under hypnosis or in therapy, rose dramatically. It seemed like a fad, but the unfortunate abductees were just as distressed when talking about their memories as people who were recalling genuine traumatic experiences.[19] Memory's a strange thing, and just as unreliable as those grainy photos of UFOs. The truth may be out there, but don't rely on finding it in your head.

## We like things more the more we see them.

Most of us are fortunate enough to be surrounded by things we like. There has to be something wrong with the woman who lives with pictures on her wall she hates and a partner she despises, who eats food she dislikes and listens to music that gets on her nerves. But do we surround ourselves with things we like or do we come to like the things we are surrounded by? Is the patriot lucky to live in the country he loves or does he love his country because he lives there?

Children have very little choice in their lives, but most of them seem happy enough. I certainly preferred my mum's cooking to that of others (except when she hid sprouts under my mashed potatoes). I remember with retrospective embarrassment having dinner at an Italian friend's house. His mum made her own pasta and I thought that I was being very charming when I told her how nice it was: almost as good as the Napolina that we ate at home.

It turns out not to be luck, nor a strange operation of genetics, that most of us appreciate our mother's cooking: being repeatedly exposed to something causes us to like it more. In one of the first experiments demonstrating this, Robert Zajonc[20] asked people to read out loud a list of nonsense words (such as Iktitaf, Dilikli and Civadra) which he claimed were Turkish adjectives. Afterwards, he asked the participants which words they thought meant something good in Turkish, and which meant something bad. Some of the words were in the list more frequently, and the more often they appeared, the more likely the subjects were to think that the words must mean something good.

This effect, that repetitive exposure to certain stimuli can increase our liking of that stimuli, has been found in hundreds of experiments.[21] Our taste for music and artwork increases as we hear and see them more often (though overexposure may invert the effect). Hearing an argument multiple times increases the chances that we'll accept it. And we may even like people more after seeing their image repeatedly (a piece of research that was presaged by numerous dictators).

## We do what we imagine others do.

To predict what other people will do, we need to have some idea of the rules that govern their behaviour. But the same rules that govern other people's behaviour influence our own actions. If we know the rules that influence our own behaviour, we ought also to know the rules that govern other people's. But in spite of this, the rules we use to make our predictions and which we apply to change other people's behaviour are often wrong: sometimes so wrong that using them has the opposite effect to that which we intend.

In Arizona, there is a fascinating national park. In this park, there are trees that have fossilised. Over time, minerals have displaced the organic material in the wood: the forest has literally turned into stone. It is so strange that visitors take mementoes. Irritated that sightseers are carting off fourteen tons of petrified wood a year, staff put up signs to try and discourage theft. But researchers suspected that the signs, telling visitors that such a huge amount was stolen, 'mostly a small piece at a time', were unhelpful.

They had a theory that, just as we mimic people automatically, in bigger things we are also swayed by what we think other people do. This theory predicts that signs telling visitors that other people are stealing from the park will increase the amount of theft. This isn't how we imagine we work, so well-meaning types create suicide prevention campaigns, eating disorder

24

programmes and high-school binge-drinking education efforts that tell their target audience just how many suicides, anorexics and drunk teenagers there are. Such campaigns have the opposite effect to that intended, and this theory might explain why.

To test their theory, they placed pieces of petrified wood along popular pathways in the park, and rotated different signs on those paths.[22] One of the signs asked ramblers: 'Please don't remove the petrified wood from the park.' Another told visitors that: 'Many past visitors have removed the petrified wood from the park, changing the natural state of the Petrified Forest', and was accompanied by a picture of three visitors taking souvenirs.

When no signs were placed along the paths, about 3% of the pieces were stolen. When walkers were asked not to take wood, without any mention of others doing so, this went down marginally to just under 2%. But when the signs told visitors of the damage being done by others (as in the park's original posters) the theft rate went up dramatically: 8% of the wood was stolen.

## We care more about one person than a hundred.

Giving money to charity makes us feel good.[23] When we decide to give money, the same reward centres in our brain are active that respond when we receive money or food ourselves, or when we punish cheats. Individuals whose brains are most active in this area also choose to give more than those who seem to get a smaller reward.

Researchers in Israel told undergraduates about either one sick child or eight sick children.[24] The students learnt that the drug needed to cure the children was expensive and they would die unless $300,000 was raised quickly (i.e. in one case the $300,000 would save one child, in the other it would save eight children). Some of the students were given the names, ages and pictures of the child(ren) while others weren't. The undergraduates then had the chance to donate money to the medical centre. The researchers found two interesting effects. When the students were given the names and pictures, they were far more likely to contribute. However, it seemed to be much harder to empathise with a group of children than with one child. The students who learnt about a single, identified child were twice as willing to contribute as those who received information that their donation would help a group of eight, even though they would be doing more good in the latter case.

But if people give more to less useful causes because their emotional attachment is greater, can the more effective charities educate people to be more rational in their giving? A US group tried this, asking participants to donate to either an individual girl at risk of starvation (volunteers saw a picture of a girl called Rokia) or to a generic cause, giving the volunteers details of a drought in Africa and describing the millions needing help.[25] The participants gave twice as much to Rokia. So the researchers repeated the experiment, but before asking the volunteers for donations they told them about research showing that people react more strongly to identifiable victims than statistics. Unfortunately, the volunteers didn't then donate twice as much to the millions of starving Africans; they donated half as much to Rokia.[26]

Men are just, women are merciful.

In 2008, the financial system collapsed, and it seemed that nearly everybody wanted to lynch a banker. At demonstrations, effigies of the evil men in suits were cursed, burnt and hung from lampposts. Banks advised their workers to stay at home or dress down while the protestors were marching past their workplaces lest the crowd get their hands on a real trader. Stringing them up wouldn't have got us our money back, but it would have given many almost as much pleasure. Why?

A group of scientists based at University College London measured the brain activity of volunteers while they played a series of games.[27] Unbeknown to those who had signed up to take part in the experiment, the people they were playing with were stooges who either played fairly or were told to cheat. The rules of the game were such that if your opposite played nicely it was possible for both of you to make money, but if he cheated he made more, at your expense.

While the games were played, the scientists gave small but painful electric shocks to the participants' hands. When seeing a fair player shocked, the same part of the brain was activated as when the participant was shocked themselves. But when a cheat was electrocuted this empathic response was completely absent.

Moreover, there is a part of the brain, the nucleus accumbens, that usually gets involved when something nice happens to you.

If you learn you've won some money, for example, the nucleus accumbens is active. It turns out that it also fires up when you see a cheat get hurt.

But there is a twist in the results of the experiment. One of the smaller criticisms of banks was that they don't employ enough women. I'm not sure whether the fairer sex burn better or worse than men, or whether you can hang them from shorter pieces of rope. However, in the UCL study they found a difference in the way men and women react to seeing someone else receive shocks. The results I described above were for men. The women in the experiment felt empathy even for the cheats (though less than for fair players). Also, the finding that seeing a cheat punished can give a buzz equivalent to earning money was only observed in men.

So what does all this mean for those hated bankers? After the crash, they should have found that they cared very much about one aspect of women's employment. They should have been desperately hoping that women got the jobs deciding what should be done to them.

Finding a rational justification for moral decisions isn't easy.

Philosophers don't have laboratories, so they do thought experiments instead. At a dinner party in Athens, or over a pipe and a glass of port in Cambridge, they imagine a scenario and work out what should happen. They then invent some rules that explain their answers for a series of such 'experiments' before concocting some more situations that pose problems for their systems of rules. One influential set of games that they use are the trolley and footbridge dilemmas.

Imagine you're a cop in Chicago in the 1920s. You get a tip-off that, in revenge for a raid on his brothel, Jimmy 'The Philosopher' Ricca has tied six men to the train tracks. You race to the scene and find five bodies trussed up in a row. You hear the train coming; the track vibrates under your feet. Running towards the screaming men, you see that the line splits and you can avoid disaster by diverting the train into a siding. But as you rush to pull the lever, you see the sixth body: gagged and tied to the rails of the siding. By now the train has roared into view and if you don't do anything there'll be five more corpses in Rosehill Cemetery. Do you pull the lever?

Most people would say that you ought to, and be quick about it. This might be seen as an example of basic moral mathematics: the lives of five people are more valuable than that of one. But a similar scenario suggests our reasoning is not so simple. Imagine instead that you've arrived on a bridge overlooking the train track. The five men are bound to the rails as before, and the train is rattling towards them. Standing next to you, looking down at the pending disaster, is an enormously fat man. As the train sounds its horn, he wipes sweat off his forehead. You size him up: he's a really big fellow. If you pushed him over the edge, onto the track, he'd certainly die, but the other five men would be saved. In this case, should you sacrifice one person to save another five?

This time, most people say no. Perhaps the difference is that in the second example you are using another person as a means to an end while in the first scenario the poor man who died was just unlucky to have been where he was: it wasn't his death which saved the others. But to find out whether this is the reasoning behind the decision we can invent a third train-track problem. Now the train is heading onto a circular route. There are six people tied to the track, five skinny men and one fat one at the end of the row. As things stand, the train will head onto the track in a clockwise direction. It will run over the five skinny men and kill them all, but the combined effect of their bodies being mangled in the wheels will stop the train and the chubby fellow will survive. However, you have the chance to switch the train so that it goes around the track in an anti-clockwise direction. The fat man will be hit first and killed but the five lean men will live. Pulling the lever in this third example seems to be another case of using the body of one human being to save five others, but now most people think that this is the best course of action.[28]

Playing around with games like these, and asking people what they would do, shows that most of us make moral decisions that can't be explained by any of the major sets of rules or principles that philosophers have invented. If we have a rational set of rules for making moral decisions, we don't know what they are: which in itself suggests they aren't rational.

Our moral decisions are primarily emotional decisions.

A group at Princeton, led by Joshua Greene, played with the same set of train-track experiments and similar, twisted moral dilemmas.[29] But instead of trying to create a Byzantine set of rules that might describe how we reason, they scanned the brains of volunteers while they answered. They thought that pushing a fat man in front of a train might be more emotionally disturbing than switching a lever that sends a train towards him.

Unsurprisingly, areas of the brain that are typically associated with emotion were more active when people were thinking about the emotional quandaries. However, the researchers also looked at parts of the brain that are usually active when making simple decisions that are neither emotional nor moral, such as which offer to use in a shop or the best way to travel to a meeting. These areas were used when making ethical decisions that were low on emotion (such as designing a vaccination program when the inoculation protects against a deadly disease but causes a small number of deaths as a side-effect), but were much less active when making the emotional ethical decisions (such as killing a single hostage to save yourself and others).

When problems are posed in a way that puts distance between ourselves and the dilemma we readily accept that the greater good should prevail. But when we have to imagine pushing a fat man to his death, smothering a child or lopping a man's head off, we answer dilemmas that are otherwise similar in a different way. It seems that we do have moral rules, but we only use them when our emotions aren't engaged. Indeed, brain-damaged patients with abnormal emotional reactions follow the mathematics more often, endorsing choices which would save the largest number of people even when they necessitated an unpleasant action such as choosing a child to die.[30] But important moral dilemmas *are* emotional, and when healthy people make moral decisions, the rules are put to one side.

What the philosophers have really been doing with their ever more complicated sets of rules is to separate the cold choices from those that engage our hearts as well as our minds. They've then been trying to encapsulate the way our feelings will affect our decisions: they've been developing a theory of emotions. But people's emotional responses differ. Because no two philosophers have quite the same responses they've been able to argue for thousands of years without getting anywhere.

## Moral reasoning is for defending choices not making them.

One of the big moral debates in the USA is the acceptability or otherwise of capital punishment. On both sides of the argument, people hold strong views. For some, the death penalty is the ultimate foundation of a just society, while for others it's the mark of a brutal, uncivilised one. For psychologists, it provides an interesting way to see motivated reasoning in action.

To do this, scientists at Stanford University gave supporters and opponents of capital punishment details of a series of investigations designed to find out whether the death penalty acted as a deterrent.[31] The studies were invented by the researchers but were designed to seem plausible. Some of the studies apparently demonstrated that the death penalty frightened off would-be killers – showing that in states that reinstituted the electric chair the murder rate dropped. Others seemed to show that capital punishment was ineffective by comparing neighbouring states and demonstrating that those which poisoned, electrified or shot convicted killers had higher murder rates.

Supporters of capital punishment found the studies that denied a deterrent effect unconvincing. But they didn't think that they found the studies unpersuasive because they already believed that the answer was wrong (which may have been a perfectly reasonable defence: they might already have had such a lot of knowledge on the subject that one more study couldn't tip the balance); they thought that the studies were poorly conducted. They were even able to pinpoint the flaws in the investigations, arguing that they didn't cover a long enough time period or took murder rates out of context when they should have looked at overall crime rates. The same supporters of capital punishment found the studies that showed the existence of a deterrent effect plausible and were able to explain how they were well designed. Yet opponents of capital punishment came to the opposite conclusion. They picked holes in the research methods of the studies that demonstrated a deterrent effect, and argued that the surveys that supported their original positions were better conducted and far more convincing. We saw earlier that we choose which politicians to back first and afterwards find reasons to support what they stand for rather than our convictions following the arguments. So it is with our moral positions.

Given two conflicting sets of information, both sides found that overall the evidence supported their original opinion. Their reasoning wasn't used for deciding whether capital punishment was right or wrong, but for explaining how the data supported their decision.

## We make better lawyers than judges.

Psychologists often make a comparison between two different types of reasoning: that of the judge on the one hand and that of the lawyer on the other. In theory, the judge and jury hear the evidence dispassionately before weighing its strength and deciding whether the accused is guilty. (But as the judge and the jury are human it's not obvious that this is what actually happens. Every lawyer will advise his or her client to turn up to court wearing a smart suit, with freshly washed hair and their tattoos covered up, implicitly accepting that impressions will in fact play a role in the judgment.)

The lawyer's role in the court is different. Given the starting point that their client is innocent, it is their job to show that the facts demonstrate this. They argue that some laws are appropriate to the case while others aren't. They apply different weightings to the evidence. They might suggest that the witnesses' memories are faulty. If none of that works, they may claim that their client didn't intend to do what he did. Ultimately, and perhaps ironically, they might argue that emotions clouded the defendant's judgment, that he was provoked and thus not responsible for his actions.

The reasoning we use in moral judgement is that of the lawyer rather than the judge. Our emotions are the client, and the brain uses all the dubious tricks of the lawyer to defend its decisions and cover the tracks of emotion's involvement.

The more damage is done, the more likely we are to find someone guilty.

When we judge somebody, it's not sufficient for us to know that they've caused harm; we also think it's important to find out whether they intended to do what they did. If a mother leaves her child alone to make a picture and comes back to find paint all over the floor, it's not enough to see that her son caused the mess to decide he deserves a telling off; the mum also needs to know whether he deliberately tipped the paint pot over or accidentally knocked it as he reached for his brush.

When the mother is deciding whether she thinks her darling boy deliberately tipped paint on the floor, it shouldn't matter whether the spill happened in the kitchen or if the mess has spread onto the new hall carpet. The harm done has nothing to do with whether it was intentional or not. Yet I know from my own childhood that the defence 'I didn't mean to, Mum!' was much more likely to be accepted when the damage was minor.

It's not just my mum who looks at the consequences of an act before deciding how responsible the perpetrator is. We all do.

Consider the following scenario.[32] A company boss weighs up the pros and cons of starting a new program. His advisers tell him that the project will increase profits, but will also harm the environment. He thinks about it, perhaps puffs on his cigar, before saying, 'I don't give a damn about the environment one way or the other. All I want to do is make as much money as I can. Get the project started.' His minions scurry away, implement the decision, make a fat profit for the company, and the environment is damaged. The question is not whether the project was justifiable, but whether the boss *intentionally* harmed the environment. Given a similar story, the overwhelming majority of people who were asked said that the chairman *did* intentionally damage the environment.

But contrast this with a different scenario. The same boss is considering another scheme. He's told that the development will make money, but will also *help* the environment. The chairman responds, 'I don't give a damn about the environment one way or the other. All I want to do is make as much money as I can. Get the project started.' The program is executed, profits are made, and the environment is improved. Did the company's boss intentionally help the environment? Faced with this account, most people say that the improvement in the environment was unintentional.

When somebody is guilty, we're more likely
to think the crime was big.

The more harmful we think something is, the more likely we are to blame the person who did it. But can it work the other way around? If somebody was clearly in the wrong, is it possible that we rate the harm that was done as being worse than if the same thing had happened by accident? If the mum saw her little sweetie-pie deliberately tipping the paint onto the floor will she imagine the stains were harder to scrub out than if sweetie-pie manages to maintain his innocence? Researchers are beginning to uncover evidence that she might.

In one experiment,[33] volunteers read a short story about a man called Frank who ate a lavish meal in a nice restaurant. At the end of the meal, he walked out without paying. Some of the participants read that Frank got a kick out of cutting and running, and often avoided his bills when he could get away with it. Other participants were told that Frank had just received a phone call telling him that his daughter had been in an accident and was badly hurt. In a state of shock, Frank immediately left the restaurant, completely forgetting about the bill.

A week later, the volunteers were asked about the story. Those who thought that Frank enjoyed avoiding his bills unsurprisingly thought him more blameworthy. But they also misremembered the size of the bill, inflating it by ten per cent. It seems that the lawyerly brain doesn't just use dubious reasoning to win the case; he's also friends with a bent cop who tampers with the evidence.

When something's really bad, we have to blame someone, even if it's the victim.


In May 2010, the Iranian cleric Kazem Sediqi gained worldwide coverage after blaming earthquakes on promiscuous women. Earlier in the year, the TV evangelist Pat Robertson gained even more attention for claiming the disaster in Haiti was sent as retribution because the islanders had sold their souls to the devil. These pronouncements are extreme examples of an effect[34] we all show.[35]

Living in an unjust world is difficult. From an early age we learn that our actions have consequences; that if we work hard and do good we will be rewarded, and if we don't then we won't. If outcomes are really arbitrary, and what happens to us is a lottery, then why not stay in bed all day?

But if the world is just, how do we explain the terrible things that happen in life, whether it's a car accident, losing our job or being robbed? How do we deal with illness? Most people would say that illness is bad luck; they feel compassion for somebody struck by disease, and the more damaging the affliction the more they feel for the victim. But if the world was fair then the nastiest diseases would only be caught by the least pleasant people. If we have an instinctive tendency to believe that the world is just then we might be inclined to disparage people who have the worst illnesses in the same way that Sediqi and Robertson found fault with earthquake victims.

Researchers conducted an experiment which found just this.[36]

They gave undergraduates some information on a fictitious disease called Haltmar's. The facts the students were given varied. Some of them were told that doctors had no way of halting the spread of the disease, while others were told that it was curable. They were then asked questions about the illness and also about an imaginary person who had the ailment. Rather than being sympathetic, the students' desire to see the world as fair was so strong that they thought less of the patient (assessing them as less brave, good and sane, for example) when they thought that his sickness was incurable. Other scientists have found similarly disturbing effects in our attitudes to people with AIDS, those struck by poverty and rape victims. We don't all have the audacity to blame natural disasters on the wickedness of the poor victims. But the same dark instinct is part of us all.

Religion and science agree: if you feel really bad about something you've done you should take a shower.

The cleaning away of filth is a centrepiece of most religions. Christians wash away sin through baptism. Sikhs also have baptisms, which they repeat after repenting for fresh transgressions. Muslims wash before saying their prayers. The Jews didn't let those considered unclean into the inner courts of the temple, and for Hindus the bathing of their whole body in rivers such as the Ganges is a major part of their faith.

Literature also makes the connection. One of Shakespeare's most famous scenes has Lady Macbeth desperately trying to clean her hands after the murder of Duncan. But what about the standard, irreligious twenty-first-century person? Surely they don't associate cleaning with the purging of sin?

In an experiment inspired by Macbeth, scientists asked participants to think about an act from their past.[37] Some were asked to think about something that they thought was unethical, and others something that they thought was ethical. They then described any feelings or emotions that they experienced. Afterwards, as thanks for taking part in the study, the volunteers received a small gift. They could choose to take either a pencil or an antiseptic wipe.

Interestingly, while one-third of those who'd been asked to think about something ethical took the wipes, two-thirds of those who'd reflected on something immoral did. None of the participants realised that the gift was part of the experiment, or that their preference was influenced by the grubby thoughts they'd had.

We re-use tools that are lying around in the
brain rather than invent new ones.

Filth and immorality are deeply connected in our language. I
searched the Internet for articles on a particularly unsavoury
far-right politician. Journalists and mainstream politicians called
him revolting, sickening, nauseating, repugnant, filthy, vile and
foul, among other things. These epithets all have something in
common: we also use them to describe food we don't like or
contaminants such as maggots or faeces.

As well as using the same words for these different types of
disgust, we also pull the same facial expressions.[38] Scientists
measured the movement of the muscle that we use to screw
our face up when we taste something foul, and found that the
same muscle was used when viewing photos of faeces or when
participants were cheated in a game. The more bitter the drink,
the more sickening the photo and the more obnoxious the
cheat, the greater the activity of the muscle.

Disgust might help us avoid bad food, but the processes that
made it good for this also made it useful for morals. Disgust gives
us a strong aversion to things, but it also has to be malleable.
Strongly smelling cheeses are unpleasant on first acquaintance,
but this revulsion can be overcome.

These are just the things we need for morality. We need a
strong aversion to immoral acts. But morals, like eating habits,
have a cultural component. We need to be able to change what
we find morally disgusting.

Rather than inventing a whole new set of tools to use for morality, the brain re-used those it had already developed for avoiding bad food and contaminants such as rotting bodies.[39] But in doing so, many of the quirks of non-moral disgust, from language to facial expression to the desire to wash after encountering dirt, were carried over to a realm where they ought to seem odder than they do.

Religions have stumbled on deep
psychological truths or they wouldn't be here.

The teachings of Christianity, Islam, Hinduism and Buddhism can't all be true. But even the wrong ones have millions of believers. People have changed their lives for all of them, died for all of them and have spent a huge amount of money building temples to fake gods before worshipping them.

To be this successful at surviving and changing the way people behave, they must be using some powerful techniques. This doesn't mean that they have super-cynical leaders who sit in a throne-room leafing through the latest psychology journals before sending pronouncements to their acolytes or amending parts of the liturgy. But religions that don't have the right mix of tools will simply die off – after all, new sects and cults are founded every year. So a study of what religions have in common and where they differ promises to reveal deep truths about ourselves even if their leaders are sometimes charlatans.

If psychologists had unlimited resources, it would be a fascinating experiment to found cults at different universities. The researchers could change aspects of their religion. They could include or neglect a weekly creed recital, promise glory to believers or death to unbelievers, insist on asceticism or hold the best parties on campus, and so on. They could measure the number of believers, and also how far they would go to protect their faith. Would their followers donate time and money to the cause, die for the cause or kill for the cause (in the interest of ethics, the researchers could supply believers with fake bullets)?

Physicists have billions of pounds for their particle accelerators and are allowed to risk the planet by potentially creating black holes in their machines. It seems unfair. Their findings can't be more interesting or important than understanding ourselves, so psychologists should be allowed a few million to go off and answer the really big questions.[40]

Fortunately, in America, evangelical Christians seem to be running the experiment for us. New churches are founded on a regular basis. Some become huge, put their pastors on television and send missionaries to Latin America. Others have to rent space in others' buildings for their tiny congregations before they fizzle out. Perhaps there's a secretive group of enterprising scientists doling out seed funding and keeping track of what does and doesn't work.

# Psychopaths are Plato's ethical superheroes.

In *Timaeus*, Plato tells a story about our creation, in which the father of the gods created a divine centre for each of us. Lesser gods finished our design. They made our heads and put our divine parts into them. To avoid polluting the divine soul too much, they placed our mortal parts in our bodies. Anger, courage and ambition were sited in the chest. The base appetites were implanted lower down, where they could cause the least disturbance. To live a life of justice, Socrates' most famous pupil argued that we must master these desires and feelings using our divine reason.

In Plato's writing it seems that avoiding wickedness and living a good life would be far easier if we didn't have emotions, desires and appetites. But we've seen that we use emotions to make moral decisions. Perhaps this is a sign that we are imperfect: our reason has become slave to our emotions. Instead of doing what it is supposed to do, and ruling over our desires, it has allowed itself to become subject to them. Plato himself pondered this possibility deeply. He thought there was a strong motivation for our reason to break free and resume its proper governance. Those divine souls that failed to rule in their first life would suffer a terrible punishment: they would be reborn in women (and if they still disappointed they would be reincarnated as animals). But is it possible to imagine somebody who isn't troubled by confusing emotions and can make their moral decisions using their reason alone?

It is, because such people exist. Psychopaths often have normal, even high, IQs. They know what is considered right and what is wrong. But they have certain emotional deficits. They don't feel empathy for others in the same way that most people do, and when they see negative images, such as pictures of mutilated faces, psychopaths don't have the same impulsive, aversive reaction.[41] They are able to make moral decisions with reason, untroubled by their emotions. About one in a hundred Americans are classed by standard tests as psychopaths. But they represent about 15–25% of the prison population, and are responsible for an even greater proportion of the most violent crimes.[42] So perhaps Plato should have been a little more positive about emotions and a little less in awe of his reasoning.

People who don't believe in free will
choose to be bad.

Having free will seems like a prerequisite for morality. If I have no control over whether I do good or bad then how can I be held responsible for my actions? It also seems clear that the choices I make must be conscious and reasoned if I'm to be held accountable for them. Unconscious processes in the brain regulate how fast children grow, but only the meanest father blames his son for growing out of his clothes. When a jellyfish stings me or a puppy bites me I don't judge them immoral, because I don't think they're capable of reasoning: they're just acting instinctively. But if the existence or otherwise of free will determines whether we think people are culpable, whether or not people believe in free will determines whether they will do things wrong in the first place.

People's belief in free will is remarkably pliable. Just reading a series of statements that assume free will, such as: 'Avoiding temptation requires that I exert my free will', or which defend determinism like: 'Ultimately, we are biological computers designed by evolution, built through genetics, and programmed by the environment', sways their attitudes. It's not clear why this should be; perhaps most people don't think about the question much. But if we think we need to have free will to have morality, do people who have been convinced they don't have it act immorally?

To find out, researchers gave volunteers an examination

practice test and paid participants $1 for each question that they got right.[43] However, the test was completely confidential, so the participants marked their own answer sheet and shredded it before taking the money from a pot. Volunteers who'd earlier read arguments for free will scored their sheet and on average took about $7 from the pot. (When examiners mark the tests, volunteers typically get about seven questions right.) Participants who had seen statements supporting determinism walked away with nearer to $11. In other experiments, people who believed less in free will were less helpful, more aggressive, and even cheated on arithmetic tests for which they weren't getting paid. These results are especially unsettling because the number of people who think that their fate is outside their control has grown rapidly since researchers began collecting data in the 1960s.[44] Yet those who believe strongly in free will do better at school, deal better with stress and are less likely to become depressed.

This leads to a moral question in itself. In this book I describe research that might convince you that we don't have free will, at least in the way that most people think of it. Am I acting immorally by telling you about it? Do I risk ruining your life and destroying your integrity? Should this book and others be banned from school libraries for fear of debasing our children? There are certainly arguments for burning the manuscript without publication, both for the harm that a deterministic world view could do its readers and for the harm that they in turn will do to people they meet.

I naturally disagree, but I'm not going to pretend I trust the arguments I could give you. They are almost certainly the product of lawyerly, motivated reasoning.

We have an emotional attachment to the
rational nature of our irrational choices.

It seems odd that thinking about our emotional reactions to
food and filth can give us an insight into our morals. Most of
us would argue vehemently that our ethical principles come
from rational thought. If you drew a line, with deep reflection
embodied at one end by Plato, and instinctive likes and dislikes
represented at the other end with a child screwing their face up
at their dinner, we believe that our morals come from the Plato
end.

But philosophers have had thousands of years trying to come
up with a framework that we, or even they, can agree does,
should or ought to govern morality. And they've failed
spectacularly.

The problem for philosophers, puffing on pipes in darkened
rooms, is that morals aren't merely theoretical: they exist in the
real world and have to be studied there. We've all felt guilty,
we've all given money to charity or stood up when a pregnant
woman needs our seat. Philosophers can argue over how an ideal
Kantian man, if he lived, would behave in such-and-such circumstances, or what a perfect utilitarian would do in some other
situation. But such people don't exist, never have and never will.
Talking about them is a parlour game, like asking how people
would breathe in a two-dimensional world or the best tactic for
playing chess if time went backwards.

For me, it's more interesting to ask how we actually get our moral ideas, when we'll act on them, and when we won't. Some philosophers agree. David Hume wrote, 'Men are now cured of their passion for hypotheses and systems in natural philosophy, and will hearken to no arguments but those which are derived from experience. It is full time they should attempt a like reformation in all moral disquisitions; and reject every system of ethics, however subtle or ingenious, which is not founded on fact and observation.'[45]

For Hume, ethics clearly belonged to the scientists. If his advice had been followed, ethicists would now be found in science departments. There would be no need to have them in philosophy departments any more than astronomers, physicists or chemists. But it is of course a moral dilemma as to whether we can put thousands of philosophers on the streets unable to fend for themselves and give their salaries to people who might actually get the job done.

Art and philosophy are how we think about things that haven't yet become a science.

Renaissance painters studied physiology and perspective. But once scientists did the job properly they moved on. Galloping horses were once painted with their legs splayed. Then photographers showed how they really ran. Old pictures of steeplechases look strange to us now.

Philosophers used to write about the nature of matter. Once physicists split atoms they had to find new things to think about.

Much of literature today is about people's motivations. What would people do in some situation? What is the moral thing to do? Now that psychologists are finding out how we really make moral decisions will writers have to find some new topic?

Most people put more time into learning to drive or use computer software than understanding how their minds work.

They're happy with a concept of their brain that's as silly as a child's understanding of how presents appear under the tree at Christmas. The child's concept works most of the time: she writes a letter to Santa and gets some of what she asks for. In the same way, our minds are forgiving and we have the illusion that we understand why we do what we do most of the time.

I'm not sure what a little girl would get out of knowing Father Christmas didn't exist. But knowing how your mind works can help you to use it more effectively. We can exploit the gap between how we really work and how we imagine we work to change our behaviour and that of others.

## PART TWO

The unconscious does what the conscious thinks the conscious does

## We don't need to be conscious to do the things we're conscious of.

Plants aren't conscious, but they still go on stretching up to the sky and scattering seeds. Worms probably aren't aware of the pleasing squelch of mud, but they go on burrowing through it.

Humans *are* conscious. We are conscious of seeing things, learning things, reaching out to touch things, deliberating ethical questions, making decisions, fancying someone, and setting goals. But consciousness isn't *needed* for any of these things. In fact, when we do them, it generally isn't consciousness doing them at all. Our conscious experience is separate from the processes in the brain that actually decide things, guide us as we reach out for things or set our goals. This explains why so many of the ways in which psychologists can manipulate us seem strange to us: if consciousness determined our behaviour we'd already know that was how we worked; but as it doesn't, we don't.

You learnt how to read this without knowing what you were learning.

I was part of a massive experiment, which, if you are under fifty, you were probably a part of too. Some years ago, English teachers stopped teaching grammar. I never learnt what an adverb is or the difference between lexical, auxiliary and modal verbs. Imperatives, infinitives, present participles, gerunds and subjunctives are all meaningless terms to me.

The astonishing thing is that those of us who were a part of this experiment can put together more-or-less grammatically correct sentences.* We can spot when somebody isn't following the main rules. A Russian learning English might, when tired of his exercises, say, 'Why not to take a break now?' I know that there's something amiss with his sentence, and I know how to correct it, but I can't tell the Russian which rules of English he is breaking.

It was only when I later learnt French that I found out about the gaps in my knowledge of English. Before the French teacher could teach us how to conjugate French verbs, she had to tell us what verbs were in English, then explain conjugation. To give us a conscious understanding of another language she had to teach us the laws which made it work, but our brains naturally learn the rules of language very differently.

*The editor who looks at this work before you do might make a harsher, better-informed judgement.

In the endnotes, I've included a test.[46] In this test, you will find that you can quickly learn the grammar of an alien language without realising what the grammar is, or even what I mean by a grammar until you've finished the test.

You know more than you know there is to know, but you know less than you think you know about knowing.

If you've ever worked for a large, bureaucratic organisation, you've probably been on 'transferable skills' courses which explain how your mind works and how to improve it. One model you might have learnt about is an unconscious competence model. You begin with unconscious ignorance (you don't know you don't know something), then you learn that you don't know something (conscious ignorance), before progressing to conscious knowledge and finally achieving unconscious knowledge (or mastery!) when you can do something automatically. I myself have been on such a course, and in fact still have the handout. This model, it tells us, represents the way we learn all skills. It also says firmly that there's no way to skip any of the steps.

But in fact, like most of what seems obvious about knowing, it's wrong. Pawel Lewicki and colleagues at the University of Tulsa showed that you can skip all the conscious steps and go straight from not knowing that there is anything to learn to knowing it without realising.[47] Usually, psychologists use naïve subjects who won't be able to guess the trickery in their experiments (first-year undergraduates are a popular choice). But these researchers used subjects that they expected to be suspicious: they were all psychology faculty.

The experimenters split a computer screen into four quadrants with a cross through the centre. An 'X' symbol appeared in one of the sections. The volunteering psychologists pressed a key to say which quadrant the mark was in as quickly and accurately as they could. An 'X' appeared elsewhere on the screen and the subjects pressed another key. There were over 4,000 trials, and it took the psychologists about three-quarters of an hour to finish.

The sequence of the display wasn't quite haphazard. In every five trials, two of the positions were randomly generated, but the other three could be predicted by a complicated set of rules. As the experiment went on, the subjects became dramatically faster and more accurate. So had the psychologists spotted the pattern?

After the experiment, the subjects were understandably tired, but keen to work out what the purpose of the task was. Almost half of the psychologists, knowing that the experimenters studied the unconscious, suspected that they'd been subliminally primed in some way. None of them mentioned the pattern at all, so the experimenters asked them specifically about the sequence of locations. Nobody came even close to working out the real underlying pattern.

You might wonder whether the psychologists' brains really did understand the pattern or whether their reaction times just got better with practice. To rule this out, the experimenters switched to a different, but similar, rule for moving the 'X' after about 3,500 trials. The response speed and accuracy of the psychologists abruptly dropped. The psychologists were aware that their performance had declined, but didn't know why. They said that their fingers had 'suddenly lost the rhythm'.

## Unconscious knowledge isn't an oxymoron: it's the norm.

As young children, we learn to walk. At first we're a little clumsy, but soon the process of co-ordinating our muscles and keeping our balance becomes effortless. But this doesn't mean that we ever understand what we're doing.

You may or may not be able to touch your toes, but you're unlikely to fall over trying. Now stand with your heels against a wall and try again. It's not possible to do. You probably know why. In a physics lesson, you learnt about centres of gravity and you know that when you lean forward you push your bottom back so that your centre of gravity is still over your feet. When you're standing against a wall you can't do this and so you'd fall forward.

If you have access to a young child, ask them to touch their toes. Kids are pretty bendy, so they'll probably do better than you (or at least me). Now ask them to try it while their heels are against the wall. Children aren't quite indestructible, and I don't want to get sued by angry parents, so make sure there aren't any tables nearby and get ready to catch them.

If we learn to walk by carefully watching what other people do, and it only slowly becomes automatic with practice, you'd expect children to know it can't be done; it's a new skill for them. But the child will almost certainly (unless someone else has got to them first) be surprised to find themselves falling over. They had no idea that they were pushing their bottom back when they touched their toes.

We learn about balance without any real understanding of what we are learning. It's only much later that we receive a conscious, physics- and anatomy-based explanation of how to remain upright.

Not thinking can be the best
way of thinking.

It's interesting that we learn things without realising, but you also have a smart, conscious brain. If you can engage your unconscious and your conscious mind simultaneously, then you might expect to learn even faster. But sadly, the conscious brain can sometimes be a hindrance rather than a help.

Researchers in Pittsburgh gave undergraduates some puzzles to solve. If you like brainteasers, you might have seen some of them before and you'd be excluded from the experiment. Here are two of them:

1. A prisoner was attempting to escape from a tower. He found in his cell a rope that was half long enough to permit him to reach the ground safely. He divided the rope in half, tied the two parts together, and escaped. How could he have done this?

2. A dealer in antique coins got an offer to buy a beautiful bronze coin. The coin had an emperor's head on one side and the date 544 B.C. stamped on the other. The dealer examined the coin, but instead of buying it, he called the police. Why?

If the students hadn't solved a problem in two minutes, the experimenters asked them to stop. Half of the students then wrote down as much detail as they could remember about how they'd been trying to solve the riddle. The other half worked on an unrelated crossword. After ninety seconds, they returned to trying to solve the problem.

You might expect that the students who described their attempts would do better. They'd had an extra ninety seconds thinking about the problem, and had attempted to structure their thoughts. But writing down their thought processes made them worse rather than better, and they were much less likely to get the answer. Their conscious brain interfered with their unconscious brain's more effective strategies.[48]

A similar effect is found when solving more practical problems. In one study, subjects were asked to choose between cars based on twelve pieces of information.[49] One of the cars was good on nine of the attributes, another on six, and the third on just three of the twelve items.

After reading the information, half of the participants were allowed to think carefully about which car they would prefer. The other half solved anagrams. The volunteers who were concentrating on the anagrams presumably weren't able to think consciously about the car options. However, they were more than twice as likely to choose the best car.

At school, a maths teacher who I took to be rather batty told me that when I had trouble completing a problem I shouldn't struggle too long over it but take a bath and think about something else. The advice was good, if a little impractical during exams. Whether you want to solve riddles, make the best choice or improve your golf swing, sometimes it's better to stop cudgelling your brain and let the unconscious do the thinking.

The way we think of learning is due to the way we are taught rather than the way we learn.

It's easy to teach the rules of algebra, the laws of gravity or how many wives Henry VIII had. Schools, universities and business training courses naturally focus on this sort of knowledge.

Communication is fundamentally conscious. Understanding why people are telling us what they are telling us, and what they think we will do with the knowledge, is a large part of why we have a model of ourselves.

But you often gain the most important skills without any conscious steps. Motor skills such as walking or playing golf, difficult language skills such as grammar, and sophisticated problem-solving skills are all driven by our unconscious; and conscious reflection can do you more harm than good.

Our unconscious can read.

In the 1950s, a marketer, James Vicary, convinced a cinema in New York to flash up the messages 'Eat Popcorn' and 'Drink Coca-Cola' for a fraction of a second during a film. He claimed that sales of Coke increased by 18%, and people ate 58% more popcorn. Understandably, people were outraged.

The *New Yorker* said that minds had been 'broken and entered'. Another magazine labelled it 'the most alarming invention since Mr Gatling invented his gun'. Regulators banned subliminal ads. The public were told that adverts for everything from cigarettes to perfume contained hidden messages. Parents of men who committed suicide claimed that they had killed themselves after hearing a subliminal message embedded in a rock song, and attempted to sue the band. In 2000, George W. Bush was accused of using the technique by flashing the word 'rats' across a picture of Al Gore for a thirtieth of a second, and was forced to say that the juxtaposition was unintentional. He wasn't trying to do anything 'subliminable'.

But a few years after his experiment, Vicary admitted that his results were unreliable and he hadn't, in fact, produced any evidence at all for subliminal persuasion. Psychologists were able to pronounce the technique a myth, and advertisers were relieved that their artistry was more valuable than broadcasting slots lasting thousandths of seconds. Conspiracy theorists continued to collect examples of what they claimed were subliminal messages in adverts, but commercially and academically Vicary had helped make disreputable what would later be one of the most interesting scientific fields.[50]

In 2008, an experiment showed beyond doubt that subliminal messages *could* affect people's motivation.[51] Participants pressed a hand grip for a few seconds when the word *squeeze* appeared on a screen. Before the command appeared, the screen showed a series of other words. Some of these were positive words (such as *good* or *pleasant*), while some of them were neutral (such as *furthermore* or *around*). Sometimes the positive words were paired with a synonym for exertion (such as *vigorous*), displayed for three-hundredths of a second, which was too short a period for the participants to even realise that they'd seen another word. On other trials the exertion word was shown with the neutral words, and in others there was no subliminal message at all.

The subjects who'd been screened the invisible message responded faster to the *squeeze* command, and gripped tighter. They hadn't seen the word consciously, but their brain had received the signal and prepared their bodies for the action they knew was coming. Even more dramatically, those who'd had the subliminal message alongside positive words squeezed more than twice as hard. When asked afterwards how much effort they'd put into the task, people in all three groups thought they'd been gripping equally hard. Not only had participants not realised that they were receiving a secret message, they didn't realise that their behaviour had changed.

Our unconscious understands the value of money.

In another series of trials, volunteers squeezed a handgrip whenever they saw a signal on a screen.[52] Each trial was worth a penny or a pound. The harder the volunteers squeezed the more of the money they got to keep.

There's an optimal strategy to playing this game. Squeeze hard when the trial is worth a lot, and only squeeze a bit when the prize is a penny to conserve energy for more valuable trials. It doesn't take a lot to work this out, and unsurprisingly this is what the volunteers did.

But the volunteers didn't know that they knew how much each trial was worth. Before each signal to squeeze, an image of a coin appeared for less than two hundredths of a second. When the volunteers were asked what they'd seen, they did no better than chance at guessing which coin was displayed. Yet their unconscious was able to see the coin, understand its value, work out the optimal strategy and send the signal to squeeze hard or gently.

We like things more the more we see them, even when we don't see them.

Without being paid, other people promote brands to us every day. Our friends might wear T-shirts bearing a little man riding a horse. Our colleagues carry back sandwiches in a bag that says 'M&S', 'Paul' or 'Upper Crust'. Their coffee cups are marked 'Starbucks' or 'Caffé Nero'. At the gym, trainers are patterned with a large 'N', a swoosh or three stripes. Brands are so ubiquitous in our lives that we barely notice them. Could they influence our choices while we're ignoring them?

An American group thought that they might.[53] They showed 126 Maryland students a series of twenty rather boring photos. In each photograph was a person going about their everyday business: having lunch, waiting at a bus stop, working on a laptop. The researchers told the participants that they would be questioned on the photos afterwards, and asked them to focus on the facial expressions of the people in the pictures.

In some of the photos, there was a bottle of Dasani water. (Dasani is a popular water brand in the USA, but not the market leader among Maryland students.) In others, the bottle had been airbrushed out. Some students saw the bottle in twelve photos, others in four, and others in none of the pictures.

After looking at the photos, the students chose a bottle of water (Aquafine, Deer Park, Poland Spring or Dasani) as a reward for taking part. They also answered questions on whether they'd noticed any brands in the photos, and specifically whether they'd seen any Dasani bottles. Most students didn't notice the product placement at all. Only 27% of those who'd seen twelve Dasani photos and 12% of those who'd seen four were able to recall doing so.

But even among the students that had completely missed the manipulation, the effect on their choices was strong. 17% of students who had seen the sequence of photos without any product placement chose Dasani. But among the students who'd seen four Dasani photos, but not noticed the brand, 22% chose Dasani. Twelve unnoticed exposures and 40% of participants wanted Dasani water.[54] The most effective adverts can be those we don't notice, carried by people who don't know they're advertising.

## The unconscious rules.

In principle, it's relatively simple to show that something we do is the result of an unconscious process. If we manipulate a group of people in some way, and their behaviour changes, we know that the manipulation had an effect. If none of the subjects can report the manipulation, or identify the link between the manipulation and their behaviour, we have demonstrated that unconscious processes responded to the manipulation and changed the participants' behaviour.

You might expect that the hard part is finding something interesting that the unconscious controls. All the things we really care about – our goals, our beliefs, our desires, our emotions, what we see and remember – seem to be, if not under conscious control, at least consciously accessible. But the reverse is true: nearly everything interesting about the way humans act is determined by the unconscious.

The unconscious determines the way we behave.

*Before reading this section, you might like to try the exercise in the endnotes.*[55]

Things we aren't aware of affect the way we treat other people. John Bargh and colleagues gave a word unscrambling test to students at New York University.[56] The students received lists such as 'apple the please rules respect' and had to eliminate a word and rearrange them to form sentences such as 'please respect the rules'. Half of the students received lists in which the experimenters had embedded words loosely related to politeness such as *respect, sensitively, discreetly*. To others the researchers gave tests containing words related to rudeness (e.g. *aggressively, bold, intrude*) or neutral words (e.g. *exercising, send, watches*). They also lied to participants and told them that there would be a second test.

When the students had finished the first test and wanted the second one, the experimenter was deep in conversation with a friend. 60% of the students primed with rudeness interrupted within ten minutes, compared to about 40% of the unprimed students and less than 20% of the participants primed with politeness. None of the students noticed the connection between words in the test, and none of them realised that the exercise could have affected their behaviour.

If the brain is a library, the mind is a lazy reader.

I'm a member of a library with a somewhat idiosyncratic shelving system. For reasons that have been long forgotten, the books on bees and beekeeping are kept next to those on archaeology. Volumes on psychology are neatly ordered next to those on magic. Because I'm easily distracted, I often visit the library to pick up something on advertising and find myself browsing through an old tome on alchemy, which somebody has stored on the shelf above. This is very good for my all-round education (and equally bad for my productivity), but it has unintended consequences. Imagine that I'm there looking for something on Ancient Egypt, and my wife has, for idiosyncratic reasons of her own, asked me to fetch her a book on social insects. She's far more likely to get one on bees than one on ants, which are stored on a different floor altogether.

The brain doesn't store books, but it does stock concepts, goals, feelings and behaviour. There isn't a little man inside our heads scurrying about fetching concepts when we need them, and our ideas aren't physically located on adjoining sections of grey matter, but some of the things our brains store are closely connected. And fetching one of them makes others which are linked more easily accessible. When I see a snake, lots of details about snakes come to mind: they have fangs and forked tongues and they hiss. But the brain also picks up the programme that readies me to run.

We might think that concepts and programmes for action are very different types of things, but it's important that the brain can make the connection between the two. We aren't designed for pure thought. Nobody ever had sex, found shelter or caught dinner just by thinking about it. We're made for doing things and any idea that can't ultimately be turned into action is biologically useless.

The library of our brain has two levels of organisation. One is hard-wired. When the architect built the place, he put the shelf for snakes next to the slot for the programme 'get ready to run'. But the librarian also uses her discretion. She notices that when I reach for the concept 'librarian' I also keep taking a book on 'women' so she puts the two close by to save me some work.

Unfortunately, it's not possible to directly ask for a layout of the stock in the mental library. If you cut the brain open you get a gloopy grey sponge, which isn't very illuminating. So how can you find out about it?

If you wanted to discover what my real library looked like, but weren't allowed inside, you might just ask me. But I might forget. Or I might be less than honest. I might be embarrassed that the books on advertising are stacked below those on alchemy and tell you that they are near those on marketing. Finally, I might not know where all the books are stacked. When I went for my volume on Ancient Egypt and then looked about for my wife's book, I found one on bees easily enough. Yet had I looked left rather than right I could have seen the collection of works on termites.

Questions on the mind are subject to the same two problems. If you ask a fourteen-year-old boy whether snakes frighten him, he might well say that they don't, even though he knows that they do. If you ask me whether I associate librarianship with women I might say of course not and even give you examples of male librarians that I've met, genuinely believing that the two concepts are unlinked in my mind.

Another way to explore the inside of my library is to send a member in for some books on archaeology and then drop them a text message asking for a book on insects. You then send another member for a novel and again text them to ask something on insects. Most of the members you've sent for archaeology books come back with works on bees, and most of those who first went to the fiction section return with tracts on earwigs. Provided that they haven't realised what you are doing, you can conclude something about the layout from this.

Psychologists use just this technique to prime people and explore their behaviour. The word unscrambling test in the last section was an example of a method of priming. First, they activate a concept in a subject's mind without them realising. Then they measure something else which might be linked to the first concept: attitudes, goals and behaviour have all been successfully modified by priming. Priming is fascinating for two reasons. Firstly, it gives us a map of the connections in our brain. But secondly, and most startlingly, it shows us that much of our behaviour is determined by our unconscious. We have no conscious access to the layout of our library. We aren't aware of the initial prime, but it still changes our behaviour. If our decision to behave in some way was conscious, as we imagine, it shouldn't be possible to change the way we act without us realising.

You don't need to know you have a goal to aim for it.

Goals seem fundamentally conscious. If you didn't know what you wanted to achieve then you couldn't accomplish it. If I didn't know that I wanted to complete this book then surely I wouldn't be here tapping away.[57] But if the unconscious controls much of what we think and do, perhaps we can have unconscious goals too.

Tanya Chartrand and colleagues used a scrambled word task, similar in design to the one described above, to prime volunteers.[58] Participants constructed grammatically correct sentences using four of five words in a list. For example, for the list 'he frugal what want did', the solution is 'what did he want'. For some of the volunteers, words invoking thrift were embedded in the lists, for others words related to prestige.

After a filler task, participants received their choice of one pair of Tommy Hilfiger socks (valued at $6) or three pairs of Hanes socks (total value $6). Only one in five of those primed with frugality chose the fancy pair, but three in five of those primed with prestige took the Hilfiger socks.

The same effect occurred with a bigger choice. Participants were placed in a lucky draw. If they won they would get a prize worth $100, but they had to specify what they would like before the draw. They could have a Timex watch (worth $22.50) plus $77.50 cash or a Guess watch (worth $75) plus $25 cash. Just 22% of thrift-primed volunteers wanted the expensive watch, but 65% of prestige-primed participants chose it and the smaller sum of cash. Yet none of the participants realised that there was a connection between the words in the lists, guessed the purpose of the study or believed that the unscrambling task could have altered their choices.

Most methods of priming are banned or impractical. In real life companies can't make us complete scrambled-word tests before going shopping. But if your child receives a wordsearch in a Christmas promotion I'd fear for your wallet.

You hear with your eyes and see with your ears.

It is common knowledge that we see with our eyes, hear with our ears, taste with our tongue and smell with our nose. But it isn't true.

In the Seventies, Harry McGurk and John MacDonald stumbled on a curious but important effect. They dubbed the syllable *ba* onto a video of a girl mouthing *ga*. When they watched the video, they clearly heard the syllable *da*. They weren't taking anything, and the effect wasn't caused by too many late nights: we're all fooled by it.[59]

There are Internet videos that play on this effect.[60] When you close your eyes and watch them, you'll hear the syllable *ba*. When you open your eyes you won't hear one thing and see another: you'll clearly hear the syllable *da*. Knowing about the trick and how it is caused won't make it go away.

In the opposite direction, the information that reaches your ears can change what you see. When a single flash of light is accompanied by a series of beeps in quick succession, we see multiple flashes of light.[61]

We have the impression that we piece the world together in our conscious mind. We have the illusion that we see and hear things through our senses. But in fact, the world is interpreted long before we're aware of it. Not only does consciousness not combine the information from our senses, it doesn't even know which senses are providing the information.

Your hand's eye is more accurate than your mind's eye.

As a child, if not more recently, you'll have seen the Ebbinghaus illusion. When a circle is surrounded by other, much smaller, circles it appears bigger than when it is surrounded by large circles.

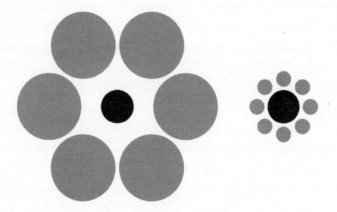

The Ebbinghaus illusion

Distorting illusions like this are fun, but they potentially make dealing with our surroundings tricky. If we don't see things the way they are, how can we manipulate them?

When we reach for something, we open our hand before we get to it. In mid-flight we separate our fingers and thumb in readiness to grasp it. When we reach for a pencil we sensibly separate them less than when we reach for a tennis ball or a box of tissues. So if someone reached for a poker chip surrounded by smaller discs you might expect that they'd open their fingers wider when reaching for it than when it is surrounded by bigger discs. When they get to the chip their fingers would be in the wrong place and they'd have to fiddle around adjusting them by touch.

But they don't.[62] Visual illusions are for consciousness. The visual system, which does useful things like guide our hand to pick something up, is different to that of consciousness, which imagines that it does such things. The system that really picks things up isn't fooled by illusions; it can't afford to be.

## The unconscious isn't simple and it isn't (just) weird.

For a long time, the unconscious wasn't studied by serious scientists. It was the preserve of psychotherapists like Freud who saw it as a dark corner of the mind doing very weird (mostly sexual) things. It was the entertainingly odd sideshow of hypnosis. It was latched upon by tricksters such as James Vicary with his 'Eat Popcorn' adverts at the cinema.

Alternatively, the unconscious did very simple and boring things like control your heart rate. It took over when you were typing or driving while thinking of something else.

The interesting part of the mind was conscious. When we made important decisions, talked to people or reflected on life we knew what we were doing. But as we've seen, most of the things we imagine to be conscious are actually done unconsciously. The question we now have to ask is how and why consciousness has pulled this confidence trick. Why do we have the conscious impression that we know why and what we are doing?

## PART THREE

You might think it's what's inside that counts. But your brain constructs the inside from the outside, whether you're looking at someone else – or yourself

## Consciously, you can't even choose to move your finger.

You might think that it is easy to demonstrate that you have conscious control over your actions. Clench your fists. Now extend one of your fingers. The left or the right, it's your choice. My betting is that you weren't surprised which finger you extended. You made a conscious decision to extend one of your fingers (or to ignore my experiment and keep reading) and then you acted on it. Consciousness seems to be where we make decisions. But unfortunately, it's not so simple: our experience of what we're experiencing isn't a good guide to what we're actually experiencing.

Imagine that I could short-circuit your brain. I could get to the bit that sends the signals to the muscles. Whichever part of the brain this is, the signal must come after the conscious decision has been made, if you're making a conscious decision. So if I told the muscle-controlling bit of the brain to extend your left finger you'd notice at least half the time. You decide to extend your right finger and your left finger stretches. You'd ask what was going on.

But if the conscious brain didn't make the decision, but only inferred that it had when your left finger was extended, then you wouldn't ask any such thing. Some unconscious part of the brain tells the left finger to move, it moves, the conscious brain infers that it must have told it to. Some unconscious part of the brain tells the right finger to move, I interfere and tell your left finger to move, the conscious brain infers that it told the left finger to move.

Scientists do have a tool for directly messing with your brain: transcranial magnetic stimulation (TMS). A TMS machine is one of the funkiest toys available to brain researchers. Modern machines look like a large donut on a stick. Scientists wave them over the head of volunteers and they emit powerful magnetic pulses, disrupting the functioning of part of the brain and effectively creating a small, temporary area of brain damage.

A team in Maryland asked participants to extend one of their index fingers when they heard a click (this was the noise made by the machine when it fired a pulse).[63] The participants did so as quickly as possible and chose which finger they wanted to extend only on the signal. The subjects couldn't see what the team was doing with the machine, and sometimes the researchers fired it away from the head. In these trials, volunteers were as likely to extend their left as their right fingers. But sometimes the researchers fired the pulse into a motor area of the brain. In these trials, responses were typically much faster, and the finger that was extended was far more likely to be on the opposite side of the body to the region of the brain that was zapped. Yet the participants had no idea that the donut was making their decisions for them; they still had the perception that they were consciously choosing which finger to extend after they heard the click.[64]

Consciously, we infer a decision to act from the fact that we have acted.[65]

We infer what other people are feeling from their expressions. We infer what we are feeling from our expressions.

Let's remember how a naïve person, the sort of person you and I used to be, imagines happiness works. Something makes them happy. Perhaps a warm summer day, a kiss from their partner, or an unexpected pay rise. This makes them happy, and they know it. They feel it directly. It's a swelling in the chest or a lightening of the heart. But if the conscious mind isn't privy to what really makes the brain tick, how might it conclude it's supposed to be happy?

I know that someone else is happy because they smile. They probably imagine that the smile came after they themselves knew they were happy, but in fact our outward expressions of emotion are one of the ways that our conscious brain works out how we are feeling.

In one experiment showing this, researchers asked participants how funny they thought some cartoons were. While they looked at the cartoons, some of the volunteers held a pen between their teeth without it touching their lips. Others held a pen in their lips without allowing it to touch their teeth. If you try this in front of a mirror, you'll see that when you hold a pen in your lips you look vaguely as though you're frowning; when you hold it with your teeth you're grinning.

The volunteers with the pen between their lips thought the cartoon was less funny than did volunteers holding the pen in their hands. Those with a pen between their teeth thought it was funniest. Simply contracting the same muscles as when we're amused (or unamused) changes how we perceive things.

Other studies reveal similar results. In one experiment,[66] some subjects shook their heads while listening to a message (ostensibly to check the fit of the headphones); others nodded. The subjects who nodded claimed to have agreed with the message more than those who shook their heads. In another experiment, subjects who sat upright in a straight-backed chair while receiving the results of a task reported being more proud of their achievement than those who were slouched in a recliner.[67]

We infer our own feelings in the way that other people infer our feelings. These results are odd, but if you smile and nod your head while reading them, you'll find them far less so.

We don't choose something because we like it, we like it because we choose it.

Our unconscious makes our decisions for us. But when it does, we do not realise that it has done so, we do not know how it has done so, and nor are we left with a gaping hole in our mind and the question: 'Why did I do that?'

One of the odd quirks in the way that our unconscious makes its choices was discovered accidentally by psychologists who set up a stall in a bargain store on a Saturday morning.[68] In pilot studies they had found that shoppers seemed to have a preference for products displayed on the right.

But the psychologists weren't interested in making lots of money, or even particularly in what changed shoppers' choices, but in how well shoppers knew what affected their decision. Shoppers who agreed to take part in their survey evaluated four pairs of stockings and chose the pair that they thought was of the best quality. Hardly anybody noticed that all the stockings were identical. Just as in the pilot study, most of them chose the stockings on the right. (12% chose those on the far left, while 40% chose those on the far right.)

But when asked why they had chosen the particular pair of stockings, shoppers didn't reply that it was because they have a tendency to like things on the right-hand side, or even that they didn't have a clue. They pointed to the knit, elasticity or sheerness of the tights. When the researchers asked the shoppers directly whether the position of the article might have influenced their choice, not only did nearly all of them deny the possibility, they looked at the interviewer as if he was mad. (The one exception was a psychology student.)

The impression we have of conscious choice isn't as well linked to how we actually make decisions as we imagine it to be. Our unconscious uses strange methods to make our choices for us. The role of consciousness is to explain plausibly why we made the decision we did in the way that someone else (with an equal lack of knowledge about how decisions are really made) might also explain our choices.

You invent the method used to solve a problem after you've solved the problem.

We can spot patterns and pick up rules unconsciously; can we also solve more sophisticated problems without awareness? And if we can, what do we experience when we do so? Norman Maier, a psychologist at the University of Michigan, designed an interesting experiment to find out.[69]

In his study, volunteers entered a large room. From the ceiling, two long ropes hung down, touching the floor. In the room were poles, clamps, pliers, extension cords, tables and chairs. The experimenter asked the subjects to tie the two ropes together. When the volunteers took hold of a rope they quickly found that they couldn't reach the other while holding it. But there were easy ways to finish the task.

Anchor one rope to a chair, place the chair in the middle of the room and bring the other cord over. Lengthen one rope with the extension cord. Pull one of the ropes over with the pole. Whenever the subjects found one of these solutions, the experimenter asked them to try and find another.

There was one 'difficult' solution that the researchers were interested in. If the volunteers fastened the pliers to one of the cords and set it swinging it was possible to catch it in the middle of the room while they were holding the other rope. Without help, most people failed to work this out.

So eventually the researchers gave the volunteers a clue. They nonchalantly walked to the window and as they did so they brushed against one of the cords, setting it swinging. This was a very helpful hint. With this cue, most of the volunteers worked it out. After an average of twelve minutes struggling unsuccessfully with the problem, they got there in forty seconds.

So did the volunteers make the connection between the experimenter knocking against the rope and their solution? Hardly anyone did. They described the idea as just coming to them, or claimed that a physics course suggested the possibility. One particularly lucid volunteer described a vision of monkeys swinging from trees across a river.

You might wonder whether the volunteers had in fact noticed the hint and directly, consciously used it to find the solution. They just lied to the experimenter so they could take the credit. But in another experiment, the researchers gave two hints. They tied a weight to the bottom of the cord and spun it. This was a pretty lousy clue and alone didn't produce many solutions. Later, the experimenter brushed the cord. After this, the volunteers quickly found the answer. They also credited the researchers with helping them. But they thought that it was spinning the cord with the weight attached which had been useful.

Stephen King uses a metaphor for the writer's mind. He has a conscious upstairs with all the things he's aware of. But when he has a problem, he sends it down to the guys in the basement to work on. Once they've solved it, they send the solution upstairs. But we can't expect our unconscious to send the answer up with a note: 'Courtesy of the backroom boys. This is how we did it.' Our unconscious revels in its hidden status. If we knew what it was doing it wouldn't be our unconscious.

We believe we want to do what we are doing, otherwise how would we explain to others why we are doing it?

Imagine that you'd agreed to take part in an experiment on factors affecting task performance.[70] For the first half hour, you put twelve spools on a tray with one hand, slide them off and then start again. Afterwards, the experimenter gives you a board containing forty-eight wooden pegs. You turn each of the pegs ninety degrees clockwise. Then you turn each of the pegs another ninety degrees clockwise and so on for another half hour. The experimenter sits nearby with a stopwatch, making notes on a piece of paper. You sigh, shuffle on your chair and get on with turning the knobs.

After this is all over, the experimenter debriefs you. You fill in a questionnaire, which asks how interesting and enjoyable you found the tasks. Unsurprisingly, most participants rated them as being rather dull. So far, the results are as boring as the tasks. But a second batch of volunteers had a slightly different experience.

They did the same tedious spool sorting and knob turning. But at the end, the experimenter asked them to do him a favour. He explained that the point of the task was to measure the impact of people's expectations on their performance. Sometimes, he explained, they tell participants that the tasks are a lot of fun before they start. But the person who usually does this hasn't turned up. The experimenter looks embarrassed. Would *you* mind doing this? He'll pay a dollar.

Most of the students agreed to help out. They tell a girl whom they think is about to do the task that it was really interesting. They are thanked and given the questionnaire. How enjoyable did they themselves find the task?

Their conscious brains might remember the sighing and shuffling, but they also just heard themselves tell somebody else that the task was fun. The measly dollar didn't justify the subterfuge. On average, participants in this second group rank the task as being interesting, two points higher (on an eleven-point scale) than volunteers in the first group. Their conscious brains mistook their own lies for real enthusiasm.

Money is the easiest motivation to understand: if you pay people less they'll enjoy their job more.

We infer why we do what we do in the way that other people infer why we do what we do. In the spool-turning experiment, participants inferred that they enjoyed the experiment because they heard themselves describing how much fun it was to somebody else. But we all know that people do things not just because they enjoy them, but also because they get paid. If we see a sports star advertising a razor blade, we don't necessarily imagine he's starring in the poster because he loves the blade so much that he feels the need to tell everyone about it.

So if you pay somebody to do the experiment, they might infer that they told somebody else the task was interesting because of the money rather than because they believed it. This is exactly what the experimenters found. When they paid participants $20 instead of $1 (not a small sum in the Fifties), they said the experiment was just as boring as it truly was.[71] This is just what other people expect: when they heard someone describe how much fun the experiment was and were told he was paid $20 to do so, they thought he was lying; when they heard he'd just been paid a dollar they thought he was probably telling the truth.[72]

The more you earn, the less other people – or you yourself – need to find an alternative, non-monetary explanation for why you do the work you do. So take a moment to feel sorry for the highly paid out there. When somebody tells you that they are a nurse or a publisher, you probably infer that person to be caring or to have a love of books. At the end of the month, provided they aren't paid too much, they probably conclude the same thing. But if you hear someone is a hedge-fund manager or an investment banker, you're more likely to deduce that they love money rather than their job. Unfortunately for the financier, however much fun his job might be (advising large companies on their biggest decisions can't be that boring), they'll infer the same thing.

If you want someone to love you, frighten
them a bit.

We make our decisions about romantic partners for reasons
that we may not be aware of. Yet once we've fallen for someone
our pulses quicken and our emotions take over, and we know
we're attracted. But if a quickly beating heart and sweaty palms
are sure signs that we fancy someone, is it possible that we can
misinterpret the message? If our heart is racing for some other
reason might we still think it's because we fancy someone?

A group in Canada went to a canyon to find out.[73] They
picked an attractive woman to survey some people crossing
bridges. The first bridge was suspended over a two hundred foot
drop into the rapids below. It swayed, tilted and wobbled as
sightseers crossed, clasping onto the handrail before taking each
step. The second bridge was wider, firmer and solidly constructed
in spite of only being ten feet above a shallow rivulet.

Whenever a young, unaccompanied man crossed one of the
bridges, the pretty experimenter approached him and asked if
he would mind helping her with an assignment for her psychology
class. She claimed to be interested in the effects of scenic attrac-
tions on creative expression, and asked him to write a short,
dramatic story for her. Afterwards she thanked the participant
and, explaining that she was short of time, offered to describe
the experiment in more detail later. She scribbled her name and
phone number on a sheet of paper and asked him to call if he
wanted to talk further.

Back at the lab, experimenters graded the stories for sexual content on a one to five scale. If the most sexual thing in the story was a kiss it garnered a three, while any intercourse rated a five, for example. The stories of men who had been crossing the high, rickety bridge were on average more than a point higher on the scale, and the men weren't just thinking sexually in an abstract way. Of those who had crossed the low, stable arch less than 10% rang the attractive experimenter, while nearly 40% of those who had been crossing the palpitation-inducing bridge called her.[74]

Because our conscious minds don't have access to why our pulse is really raised or our cheeks are flushed, it can mix up fear and lust. Yet as romance is a social emotion, the brain has to rely on the cues of consciousness to decide what to do. Perhaps teenage boys aren't quite as stupid as they seem when they take their dates to horror flicks rather than wishy-washy romcoms.

If you ask a man what he likes in his partner, he won't know; and he probably doesn't understand how he ended up with her in the first place.

We saw in the first part of this book that we make our romantic choices for peculiar reasons that we're not aware of. But most of us aren't aware that we aren't aware of the reasons why we chose our partner. We still have a concept of an ideal man or woman, and we're able to list attributes of our partner that we love. This mismatch is hard to explain. Is it that we make our choices unconsciously and then invent reasons that explain them, and believe that these justify our initial decision? A Swedish team found striking evidence that this is exactly what happens.[75]

They showed volunteers a series of pairs of cards, on each of which was a picture of a female face. The volunteers quickly chose the picture they found more attractive, were given the card and asked to explain why they picked that woman. However, sometimes they switched the cards before handing them to the volunteer.

About four-fifths of the time, the subject didn't notice the switch. This in itself is remarkable. When participants were asked after the experiment whether they'd have spotted the double-card ploy, the overwhelming majority said that they would have. Since the card-swap experiment, the researchers have shown that they can get away with switching teas and jams in consumer tests and most people don't notice the mismatch between their original choice and the one they receive, even when the tastes and smells are very different.

For our purposes, however, the experiment allows us to directly find out what happens when people have to explain a choice that they didn't consciously make. Do they admit that they can't explain their choice? Do they laugh nervously, realising that something odd's happened even if they can't work out what? In fact they do neither of these things. They answer with the same level of confidence as people who received their chosen card, and with the same amount of detail to support it. Sometimes they even give explanations which can't possibly have been relevant, telling the experimenter that they liked the girl's earrings when their real first choice wasn't wearing any.

If scientists can trick us in such a crude way, and we still hold that we made the selection for reasons we know about, then it's not so surprising that one part of our brain can make decisions for us and let us believe that we made them on different grounds. You might have met your *inamorato* or *inamorata* while abseiling, and they might have been wearing a red jumper, but you may still believe that their infectious laugh was the thing you fell for.

Culture is possible because we do what others do and believe we want to do what we do.

If you or I lived in a different time and place, we would think and do very different things. This would be true of important things such as whether we believe a particular god exists and what he expects from us, our attitudes to slavery and sex, and whether we think it is right to throw a woman on the funeral pyre of her husband. It is also true of lesser things: even the types of music we listen to in private and the pictures we hang on our own walls are a product of the culture we live in. It is hard to believe now, but there once existed a generation of men who generally believed that purple shirts and flares looked good.

Few of these differences between cultures are due to some factual discovery that changes the way we think. It can't be that a convincing argument takes hold and spreads: we've seen plenty of evidence that arguments are for defending our choices rather than making them. If you were transported back in time three hundred years, I doubt you could write a treatise that would convince people to stop slavery, or indeed make the English eat spaghetti for dinner.

But we have seen experiments that show us how cultures form. They explain why the differences between what people around us think and do are far smaller than the similarities, even as they are radically different from what other societies have thought and done.

We do what other people do. We mimic their gestures

unthink

automatically, we choose bottles of water that we see other
people drinking, we litter our surroundings when we see
other people have done so and we re-use our towels when we
hear that other people do. We do so automatically and also
with full knowledge.[76] Try standing up in a packed church when
everybody else is kneeling, wear your pyjamas to your local
restaurant, or cheer for the opposition during an important
match . . . if you dare.

Secondly, we underestimate the impact of other people on
our behaviour and come to believe we want to do what we are
doing. Once we've smiled, chosen the water, or explained to
somebody else that a boring task is interesting, we infer that we
are happy, like that water or enjoyed the task.

Finally, the attitudes we infer from our behaviour change our
future behaviour. Once we've conformed in some small way,
such as signing a petition or wearing a supportive badge, we
are more likely to agree to work for the cause in a big way.[77]

So we do what other people do, we believe we want to do what
we do, and our beliefs about what we want to do change what we
do. We become like the people around us. We come to share their
tastes, their opinions and their priorities. Human life is social life,
and our brains are wired to help us fit in.

104

Two brains are as easily tricked as one into believing that they know what they are doing.

It might not feel like it, but your brain is split into two distinct halves. The left half of your brain controls your right hand, receives images from the right side of your visual field and constructs sentences. The right half of your brain controls your left hand and receives images from the left side of your visual field. The two halves of your brain communicate with each other, and one of the main ways they do so is through a bundle of fibres joining them called the corpus callosum.

For some patients with severe epilepsy that can't be treated by drugs, cutting the corpus callosum can give some relief. These patients give us a fascinating insight into how our conscious brain constructs its world.[78] When patients wake from the operation, they don't feel that they now have two independent brains. They don't experience two consciousnesses. Their sense of self doesn't fundamentally change. But it is possible to communicate with one half of their brain without the other half understanding.

In one experiment, researchers showed two pictures to a split-brain patient. In the right half of his visual field (so the left half of his brain) he saw a chicken's claw. In the left half of the visual field (the right half of his brain) he saw a snow scene. The researchers then asked him to choose picture cards that went with what he saw. With his right hand (left half of brain) he chose a chicken. With his left hand he selected a shovel.

The researchers now asked him to explain his choices. Remember that the left half of the brain constructs sentences. So it was easy for him to explain that he chose a chicken to go with the chicken claw.

But what about the shovel? The left-hand side of the brain only saw the chicken's claw. It now knows that the left hand chose a spade. If the conscious brain makes decisions, or has direct access to the decision maker, this must be a mystery to the left brain. But if the conscious brain doesn't do any such thing, but only infers what the decision must have been, then it won't. It just has to work out what the connection is and then adopt the decision as its own. The patient won't be any the wiser, nothing unusual will have happened, and he won't experience a splitting of his brain into two halves.

The patient's response to the experimenters was, 'Oh that's simple. The chicken claw goes with the chicken, and you need a shovel to clean out the chicken shed.' His reply seems very odd to us. How could he not have realised that he didn't know why he chose the shovel? But that's how we all work. The unconscious brain makes decisions. The conscious brain invents reasons for those decisions. We never notice that those reasons are merely confabulations, and we retain a sense of an integrated self.

We can see without being conscious of seeing, but we can only explain what we see with consciousness.

A strange condition known as blindsight gives us insight[79] into what vision would be like if it wasn't connected to consciousness.[80] People with blindsight have suffered brain damage in part of their visual system. Afterwards, they are apparently blind in a large part of their visual field. Such patients were initially a puzzle. When scientists studying vision destroyed a similar region in monkeys' brains, the animals didn't seem to have lost their sight. But when you want to find out whether a monkey is blind, you can't ask it. You measure whether their pupils follow movement. Can they grasp objects? They could.

So researchers began studying the human patients in the way they'd assessed the monkeys. The humans couldn't do everything that a fully-sighted person can. You wouldn't expect them to: they'd suffered severe damage to their visual system. But they could point to objects, which they were unaware of seeing. They could grasp objects, holding their fingers in the right way before they got to them, even though consciously they didn't know where the object was. They could 'guess' in which direction a shape was moving. They were able to post objects through a slit at the right orientation. They could even respond to cues: reacting to arrows they thought they couldn't see.

If I saw you do any of these things, I'd assume that you knew what you were doing. You were aware of the objects you were grasping or pointing to. You'd seen the arrow, interpreted the symbol and shifted your attention to where the box was about to appear.

But these patients were blind. Their unconscious brain received visual information, which it could act on. But their conscious brain didn't get this information. People with blindsight can't infer that they're deliberately pointing to an object; they can only infer that they're guessing.

This is what our conscious brain is always doing: guessing what the unconscious is thinking. But unlike people with blindsight, we have enough information from our senses that our guesses are usually good and we perceive ourselves as actually knowing why we're doing what we're doing.

We understand our own beliefs in the same way that we understand other people's.

People with autism have what Professor Baron-Cohen, of the University of Cambridge, describes as 'mindblindness'.[81] They have difficulty attributing minds to people in the way that most of us do automatically. He showed this in what has now become a classic experiment with two dolls.[82] One of the dolls is called Sally and the other is named Anne. Sally has a marble and she places it in a basket. She then leaves the room and while she is away Anne moves Sally's marble. She takes it out of the basket and puts it in a box. Now Sally returns. Where will Sally look for her marble? From the age of three to four years,[83] most children can work out that Sally will expect her marble to be in the basket where she left it. If you have access to young children, you can try the experiment yourself. (Just tell their mum you are playing with her kids rather than experimenting on them.) But much older autistic children fail the test. They know that Anne moved the marble into the box, and predict that this is where Sally would look for it too. They aren't able to understand that Sally can have a false belief (or at least could if she wasn't a doll).

It's important to note that the way we solve the Sally / Anne question 'correctly' is by assuming that Sally is very similar to ourselves. We assume that her memory is good enough to remember where she put the toy a few minutes ago. Because we've only seen Anne move the toy once, our best guess is that she only occasionally moves it and Sally can't have expected her to. But these aren't obvious assumptions. When I was a child, I used to leave my toys wherever I last played with them. Yet when I wanted them again, the first place I looked was in the cupboard even when I hadn't seen my mum put them away.*

Autistic children have another deficit in their ability to understand minds. They can have difficulty appreciating that their own knowledge changes and that they too can have false beliefs. Researchers showed children a Smarties box and asked them what they thought was inside.[84] Unsurprisingly (and perhaps a little hopefully) the children said that they thought sweets were inside. The Scrooge-like scientists then opened the box to show them that the tube in fact contained a pencil.

Now the researchers asked the disappointed children what another child, seeing the box for the first time, would think was inside. Consistent with the Sally / Anne experiment, autistic children failed to realise that another child would expect to find Smarties in the box rather than pencils. But the researchers also asked the children what they themselves had thought was in the box before it was opened. Non-autistic children (over the age of about four) remembered that they had thought they were going to see sweets, but most autistic children claimed to have always known that there was a pencil in the box. Other studies have shown that this isn't simply a case of autistic children thinking that they can get away with lying: their understanding of their

*But even if you realise this, you can still work out that the experimenter expects you to make certain assumptions and will pass you on the test only if you say that Sally will look in the basket, which means that you've made an inference about the experimenter's belief about your belief about Sally's belief about where her doll is, and you ought to be given a gold star for your theory of mind.

own mental states really is such that they don't appreciate the fact that their knowledge has changed.

These experiments aren't just interesting because they tell us about autistic children, but also because they suggest something about how we *all* work. If the same defect causes a problem in understanding other people's minds and understanding your own mind, then it seems that we might use the same mental systems to comprehend both ourselves and others.[85]

We find it as hard to empathise with ourselves as we do with other people.

I've never taken heroin, so I find it hard to understand how addicts can live on the streets, steal from their family or prostitute themselves so that they can inject themselves with a drug that will probably kill them. But junkies themselves underestimate how powerful their addiction is when they've just shot up.

The researchers in this study recruited addicts undergoing treatment with the heroin substitute BUP.[86] They gave the addicts the chance to swap extra doses of the drug for money, making their choice on one day and receiving either the drug or the cash in five days' time. The patients had been addicts for an average of eleven years, so they had all experienced craving and satiation before, and just to make sure, the experimenters played with their doses in the weeks before the study, subjecting them to eye-dilating withdrawal symptoms and double doses.

Just before taking their top-up dose of BUP, the patients required an average of $60 to forgo an extra dose in five days' time. But when making the choice shortly after their hit, they were willing to trade it for $35. This is an astonishing failure of imagination on the addict's part; after all they'd been experiencing cravings only a few minutes before.[87]

This is just an extreme example from a plethora of experiments demonstrating that we have an inability to empathise with ourselves in the future or to appreciate what we were feeling in the past.[88] Hungry people choose to receive fattier snacks in a week than those who've just eaten (don't go shopping on an empty stomach). Volunteers sign up to drink more of a disgusting drink in a week's time than they would consume on the spot. Pregnant women are less likely to want anaesthetic during childbirth when making the decision a month before labour or a month after labour than when they make the choice during the actual birth (and this goes for women who've already had children as well as new mothers).

We are as bad at predicting what we will do in the future as we are at predicting what others will do now.

Because we use the same methods to understand ourselves as we do other people, we make the same sorts of mistakes about both. It would be nice if the methods we used were very good at predicting what we will do, but they are flawed. We believe consciousness is the centre of rationality – and perhaps it is, because we often underestimate the role of emotions on ourselves and others.

How good are we at predicting, for example, whether our peers are willing to embarrass themselves for cash? To find out, researchers split a large lecture theatre into two.[89] Half of the students received a green form. They learnt that the lecturers wanted some of them to mime at the front, pretending to be, among other things, a basketball (the ball itself), Scotch Tape or a computer. Students who agreed to perform would be paid $5. The other half received a white form. They were asked to predict what fraction of those with green forms would sign up.

Given the arguments of this book (and the title of this section), you might predict that those students sitting safely on their lecture-hall benches with white forms would overestimate the willingness of their peers to entertain them by miming. You'd be right. Those who weren't being asked to perform thought that nearly half of the others would, while just one in seven of those who risked being chosen to play a basketball accepted the money.

But the students didn't just have difficulty empathising with other people; they had the same deficit in empathising with themselves. They weren't any better at predicting whether they would be prepared to do something embarrassing, such as telling a funny story at the front of the lecture hall, in the future. One third of the students agreed to tell a story for $2 in a week's time. But when the day came, only one in eight of them were willing to actually get up and tell their anecdote. The threat of having to do something in a week isn't very scary now and so the students underestimated the impact of the fear they would experience, just as they underestimated other people's qualms.

But you can see fear on someone else's face. And usually when everybody else is afraid you should be too. When we see other people being frightened, we use this to determine how frightened we ourselves should be. The experimenters showed the students a reliably frightening clip from *The Shining*. Now the students were able to understand fear. Their willingness to sign up to tell an anecdote in a week dropped dramatically. Suddenly it was much closer to the rate of students willing to tell the story there and then.

We can't understand ourselves by looking inwards, but we sometimes can by looking at other people.

## Arguments are used for defending choices, not making them.

We don't have conscious access to our real decision-making processes. But we do have access to a model that is very good at explaining our own and other choices. A 2002 German experiment shows just how far we will go to make our choices consistent and how we take on board as beliefs all the steps we think we need.[90]

The German researchers asked volunteers whether they thought Germany should be given a permanent seat on the UN Security Council. Before asking them, they gave the volunteers some moderately persuasive arguments for membership: it would help German reunification, many UN institutions are based in Germany, and it would indicate international appreciation of Germany's efforts. Half of the volunteers were told that the arguments were made by Gerhard Schröder, the other half that Edmund Stoiber was making the case (at the time, the two politicians were running against each other for Chancellor).

Participants who supported Stoiber thought that the arguments were stronger when they believed he'd made them than when they thought Schröder had. Those who preferred Schröder thought his arguments were stronger. Afterwards the volunteers were asked not about the strength of the case they'd heard but about whether they themselves thought that Germany should have a seat on the Security Council. Those who'd just heard arguments from the politician they supported were more in favour than those who hadn't. They'd been persuaded.

If we're at all logical, it shouldn't make any difference who makes the arguments: either they're valid or they're not. We ought to choose politicians with the best plans. Instead we pick our policies once we've selected our leader. We're back to front.

It's sometimes said that you can tell when a politician is lying because his lips move. But once we've chosen a political candidate we have a remarkable capacity to deceive ourselves.

Our inability to imagine setting an unconscious goal, thinking an unconscious thought or making an unconscious decision tells us that our imagination is weak, not that our unconscious is limited.

What would you like most in the world? Vast wealth? A gorgeous partner? A brilliant intellect? If I offered it to you, but the price was that you had to give up your conscious awareness, would you make the swap?[91]

Most of us wouldn't. What's the point of having a flash car if you're not aware of the wind in your hair as you drive your fabulous boyfriend or girlfriend through the countryside? Where would be the pleasure in anything if you couldn't *feel* it?

But a question that's not as obvious to ask, but much harder to answer, is: what is the point of consciousness? Why are we aware of the wind in our hair or the curves of a beautiful car? Why did evolution grant us this wonderful, but perplexing gift?

PART FOUR

Minds don't exist, but they are still useful

To understand ourselves, we have to understand how we understand other people.

We're now at the point in the tale where the moustachioed detective waddles in to tell us whodunnit, howtheydunnit and whytheydunnit. 'Why are we conscious?' he muses, piercing the nervous occupants of the room with his sharp eyes.

In the course of a good old-fashioned mystery, it usually turns out that all the obvious suspects are red herrings. So it is with our story.

Consciousness isn't the think tank of the brain where we do all our deep and hard thinking. This suspect has a solid alibi. We often do our best thinking when consciousness is elsewhere. We were fooled into thinking that consciousness did our thinking because it knows the solutions and has a plausible, but ultimately misleading, set of workings for how we solved the puzzle.

Consciousness doesn't tie together all the other things that the brain is doing. Consciousness certainly has access to some of the things the brain does and information from our senses, but it is missing many of the rules and pieces of information that we actually use. The vision that controls our hand isn't the same one that enters consciousness. Consciousness doesn't notice the mimicking that makes us like someone, realise that we choose stockings from the right-hand side of a display, nor even know the goals that drive our behaviour.

It doesn't make sense for the bit that ties the things together in the brain to tie the wrong things together.

Finally, consciousness isn't the decision maker in the brain. It doesn't decide the little things, like which finger to move, and it doesn't decide the big things, such as who to love or whether to push somebody onto the train tracks. But the false trail leading to this suspect is perhaps the hardest to discard. The maid pipes up from her corner of the room, 'It's all very well saying that consciousness doesn't make these decisions. We've been tricked. Fair enough. But you haven't proved that consciousness doesn't make *any* decisions. Perhaps we haven't looked hard enough.'

The maid is in good company. Many scientists' reaction to early research that the unconscious did something or other was to maintain as a base case that all the important decisions were taken by the conscious brain and the experiments were showing quirky exceptions. But after lots of experimentation, nobody has yet found a class of decisions that are definitely taken by the conscious brain and not the unconscious brain. Conversely, whenever anybody has proposed a particular type of decision that consciousness makes, somebody else has come along and shown that the unconscious can do it just as well.

But in the twists and turns of the results we've looked at, there are enough clues for us to solve the mystery.

It's not a trivial case. It is what Sherlock Holmes would certainly have called a three- or even four-pipe problem. As we light our first pipe, we should turn over in our brains (conscious or otherwise) some of the most puzzling of the leads.

We've found that the unconscious does many of the things we imagine we do consciously. But we've also seen how the unconscious maintains its disguise. What we experience in consciousness is inferred from the outside in: consciousness invents its own role in the way that we work out what other people are thinking.

In this part of the book, we'll find that the clues lead us to a social theory of consciousness. We'll find that for humans to work the way they do, they need to work out what other people are working out about them, and one of the ways we do this fits well with what we know about consciousness. Consciousness isn't for understanding ourselves, it's for understanding other people. We'll find that having consciousness helps us make decisions, if it didn't it would be useless, but it doesn't make them itself – in the same way that a sommelier might influence our choice of wine but doesn't make our decision for us.

We can only deal with other people by reading their minds.

Humans live within a tremendously complicated social network. To be successful, we have to be good at predicting what other people will do. Whether you're negotiating with your boss, winning the heart of a lover, or trying to make your son go to bed, you need to be able to guess what is going on in their mind and how they will respond to what you do.

Imagine that you're wasting time at work, chatting to a colleague. He looks past your shoulder, stops talking and turns hurriedly back to his task. From this you're probably able to infer that he's seen your boss is close by and believes he'll be in trouble if he's caught talking to you. From his actions you've understood what's passing through his mind and worked back to a probable cause, which you can use to adjust your own behaviour. If your workmate has any concern for your skin as well as his own he will look at you to see if you've got the message: he'll read your mind to see whether you've read his.

You do all this mind-reading in a matter of seconds, but if you couldn't do it yourself, people who could do it would seem magical. In fact, everybody would be completely unpredictable. For, as we'll see, one of the main ways we have to predict and influence people is to attribute minds to them. From people's behaviour, their expressions and what we say, we infer the presence of minds driving their behaviour. We then use these inferred minds to predict what they will do.

To make predictions about other people, we need to model them.

If you hold this book (or your e-reader) in the air and let go, you won't be surprised by what happens next. You have a model of what will happen, which allows you to make a prediction before doing the experiment.

There are at least two aspects to using this model. Firstly, you know a set of rules that can be applied to the situation. You know that objects that are heavier than air fall towards the ground. Some objects fall straight down, others twist or flutter on the way. You know that when things hit the ground they typically make a noise, and that some of them deform, bounce or roll.

Secondly, you use specific information about the objects to calibrate your model and choose which rules to apply. How heavy is the book? How far above the ground are you holding it? Is there a draught? Is the floor carpeted? At what angle are you holding the book?

The combination of rules and specific knowledge is necessary for us if we want to apply our model and predict what will happen. So it is with people. We have general rules about how people will behave in different scenarios. We assume that most people can see things, want things, know things, feel things, do things. We fill in the details from what we observe. From where people look, we can fill in the details of what they see. From what they say and do, from their facial expressions, from what they wear, from how they've behaved in the past we fill in the details of their desires, their emotions, their temperament and more. We create a model of their minds.

We then use this parameterised model to predict their behaviour. Just as wine glasses rarely flutter to the ground, angry people don't generally chuck children under the chin.

We don't know how we or other people work; we can only model minds.

Different people have different ideas about how a thermostat works. Some people think that when you turn the thermostat to thirty degrees the radiators will be hotter than when you turn it to twenty degrees. They believe that you are telling the thermostat that you are very cold when you turn it up high and the system works harder to make you warmer.

Others think, more accurately, that whether you turn the thermostat to twenty or thirty degrees the radiators will be equally hot. But the radiators will turn off when the room (or at least the part of the room with the thermometer) hits the desired temperature. This is a different model of how the heating system works. It is a better model and makes better predictions about what will happen.

But both are just simplified models of what a heating system actually does. To use them and get warm you don't need to know how the electronics of the thermostat work or how the boiler heats and pumps the water. The person with the better model is more likely to be cosy on cold nights and save electricity on warm nights, but with either model you are better off calling an engineer when the system breaks.

In the same way, our model of what makes us happy and

why somebody else is cross is flawed. It's simple enough to use and complicated enough to be useful. But it is not the truth.*

---

*The same is true of your model of the falling book. Few of you will have solved Newton's equations to predict what would happen to the book, and fewer of you will have applied Einstein's theories (Newton was wrong). You will also have parameterised your model incorrectly: you didn't use the exact weight of the book or the precise viscosity of the air. Yet in spite of using a flawed model of how things fall and having inaccurate information, the motion of the book was still broadly what you expected: the book didn't float to the ceiling, roll along the floor or start talking to you.

A model doesn't have to be right to be useful.

Imagine a simple robot. It looks like a brick on wheels. It has two light-detecting sensors: one at the front and one at the back. When light falls on the front sensor, the motor attached to the front wheels drives them in a forward direction. It drives them faster the more light hits the detector. When light falls on the back, another motor drives the rear wheels backwards.

To model and predict the behaviour of this robot is easy. It's a light-seeking robot. It has a goal: to move to brighter places.

We can use all the machinery of our minds to build a model of the robot, and work out what it will do.

The robot can have false beliefs: if there is a bright patch obscured by a dark area, it will never move to the bright patch because it believes that it is darker in that direction and so decides to move away. You can fool the robot, using a torch to draw it into a dark pit, or help it across the dark area to the bright patch. Without any knowledge of the robot's circuitry, its capacitors and resistors or the way the motor's battery works, you can predict what the robot will do and manipulate it.

The model is, of course, wrong. The robot doesn't have goals, it doesn't have desires, and it can't be mistaken in its beliefs because it has no beliefs. There's nothing in it capable of making a decision.

The nature of models is that they are wrong. Physicists used to model atoms as little things jiggling about with electrons spinning around them. This is not now scientists' best model, indeed they have proven it to be wrong, but the model allowed earlier scientists to predict much about electricity and heat transfer, and aided in chemical manipulations. In the same way, our models of other people's minds are wrong. Not just in a particular instance, but in a fundamental sense: such minds probably don't exist. We don't have goals, desires or intentions in the way that we imagine we do. However, if the model helps us predict things about other people's behaviour and we are able to use these predictions such that our own actions are more adaptive, then it is useful to have the model.

If you talk to yourself you're mad. If you talk to your computer you're normal. If you talk to your car it's time to get a new one.

The most powerful technique we have for predicting what other objects will do is the invention of minds. We endow those things with beliefs, desires, knowledge and emotions, and use the model we so build to predict what they will do next. This technique was created for predicting what other people will do, but as it is so much more sophisticated than anything else our brains do we use it even for non-humans.[92]

A friend of mine has an old Mini. When it's cold it sometimes stalls, so she lets it rev a little in the garage before she drives it. 'Are the old bones warmer now?' she asks. 'Shall we go?' As it tries to accelerate on the slip road she whispers to it, 'Come on, old girl, we can do it. That's right.' I feel quite left out of the conversation.

As I try to work out how best to write this paragraph my virus checker pops up in the corner to tell me it's doing its job. I ask it why it has to behave like a child, constantly reminding me of its existence while I'm trying to concentrate. When the machine freezes on me, I swear at it and tell it to behave. I have a dysfunctional relationship with my computer, and I'm sure it's out to get me.

Scientists have found that one of the main predictors of whether we will attribute a mind to an object is whether we control it: the technique of attributing a mind to something and making predictions from that model is an adaptation we have for understanding things we don't have power over. For example, when ball bearings jump about in a magnetic field and we have the switch for the magnets, we don't personify them. But when the experimenters hid the switch, participants started describing the ball bearings as fighting, kissing or not wanting to stay still. They gave the ball bearings goals, and to have a goal you have to have a mind.[93]

We only need to predict the behaviour of things we don't control. So people with new Porsches don't generally talk to their cars, and if my computer worked as I wish it would, I wouldn't talk to it.

To read other people's minds we have to read our own in the way they read ours.

To predict and influence what other people do, we have to build a model of their minds.[94] But to do this, we also need to be good at working out what other people think is going on in our own minds.

Imagine that I stand on your toe. I need to know how you will react. I need to know what you're thinking. But the answer will depend (in part) on what you think went through my mind when I stood on your toe. If you conclude that it was deliberate, you might hit me and I have to get ready to defend myself. If you infer that I was just clumsy, I'll probably get away with an apology. So to know what you're going to do, and therefore what I should do, I need to know what you think I'm thinking.

To build the best possible model of your mind, I also have to build a model of my mind as you model my mind. Your model of my mind has to be a part of my model of your mind. This model of our own mind as other people will model us is the foundation of what we are conscious of.

Humans have eyes and ears; we don't have high-resolution brain scanners.

When I try and read your mind, I have to base my answer on things that I can observe. Is your face red with anger? Are you pulling your fist back? Do I know you to be hot-headed from your past actions?

You have to do the same. Do I look guilty or aggressive? Do you know me to be clumsy? Belligerent? Did I look down at your foot before I stepped on it? Am I smartly dressed or wearing a Hell's Angels bandana? If I'm going to work out what you think I'm thinking, and therefore what you'll do, I need a model of my own mind that is similar to your model of my mind.

Importantly, my model of my mind must make all the mistakes that you will make. It must be influenced by my stance. By how people have interpreted my face in the past. By the clothes I wear. Even by the colour of my skin. Humans have eyes and ears; we don't have high-resolution brain scanners. So our model of ourselves has to be flawed. Rather than working out what I'm thinking from the actual activity in my brain, this model has to infer what I'm thinking from the outside: from what you can also observe.

My model of your model of my mind is consciousness.

My model of your model of my mind has to be mistaken in the ways that you are mistaken: it has to rely not on my actual thoughts but on my behaviour, my facial expressions, and what I say to work out what I am thinking. We have already seen that we have such a model. In fact, it forms the basis of our conscious experience.

Such a model should infer that I am happy from my facial expressions, and that I am proud from my posture, and this is, as we discovered, how our conscious experience of emotions forms. Such a model should infer what I like from what I do and how much I am paid to do it, and this is how we form our conscious attitudes. Such a model should infer that I chose to move a finger because I did so, and this is what we found consciousness inferring. Such a model should work out how I solved a problem completely separately from how I actually solved a problem, and this is what we found in consciousness.

Our conscious experience is separate from how we actually decide to do what we do, and infers our emotions, desires and thought processes from the outside in because that is what we need from a model of ourselves as others model us.

We can be most unjust when we think we are fair.

What matters most in judging whether a little girl is good at school work: her exam results or where she lives? Researchers from Princeton University conducted a simple experiment which gives an uncomfortable answer to this question.[95]

In the experiment, participants watched a short video about a girl called Hannah. Half of them saw Hannah in a deprived area of run-down homes; they learnt that her father was a meat packer with little education. The other half saw a wealthier Hannah playing in a tree-lined park and possessing a lawyer as a father. When experimenters asked the participants to predict her grades, there was nothing to choose between their answers. So far, so comfortably boring.

But the experimenters showed other subjects a longer video. The first part of the video showed Hannah in the same rich or poor background. The second part of the video was the same for all participants. It showed an examiner asking Hannah a series of questions on maths, reading and science. She wasn't obviously brilliant or terrible. Given that the first part of the video didn't affect the answers of other volunteers, and the second part of the video was the same for all participants, you might predict that all of those who watched the video would guess similar grades for Hannah. But you'd be wrong.

When watching the extended videos, participants who thought that Hannah was from a poor background predicted that she would get poorer grades than those who thought Hannah was middle class.

The question in the first experiment seemed a silly one: participants knew they didn't know how good or bad Hannah was. But in the second, they'd seen her being tested. They thought that they knew poor Hannah was dim and rich Hannah was smart. They believed they were fairly assessing how Hannah answered the questions in the test with no idea that their brain was applying a stereotype.

Our conscious model of our self is primarily for adjusting how we are perceived. When only Hannah's background was shown, any observer – and participants' own consciousness, which aims to replicate what an outside observer would infer – could tell that any response to the question about her ability would be based on a stereotype. But when the test and the background were shown together, participants' own conscious models inferred that the decision was made based on Hannah's answers. Again, consciousness doesn't know the real reasoning behind proposed decisions, so it had no reason to infer that a stereotype was used or to advise the decision maker in the brain that its proposed answer was inappropriate. Only through controlled experiments were scientists able to demonstrate the real driver of participants' answers.

Our conscious attitudes can only affect our behaviour when other people can work out our attitudes from our behaviour.

Stereotypes are a particularly rich area in which to examine the operation and usefulness of our conscious models of ourselves. This is because people's conscious attitudes, and knowledge of what is acceptable, differ from their automatic, unconscious use of them. Most people claim not to believe or use negative stereotypes. However, when studied in quick, reaction-time type experiments – which are far too fast for our slow, conscious minds to be consulted[96] – experimenters find that most of us do use stereotypes to make judgments, even when we belong to the stereotyped group.[97] The use of stereotypes also shows up in slower experiments (such as that with Hannah) when participants' behaviour can be attributed by themselves and others to alternative causes.[98]

Consciously, we have many egalitarian attitudes, but our automatic behaviour can still be non-egalitarian, without us ever inferring that we're prejudiced. The following experiment demonstrates this neatly.

Uhlmann and colleagues[99] gave subjects in the USA a moral dilemma based on the train-track experiments we looked at earlier. Would participants push a large man in front of a train track in order to save a hundred lives? The twist in their experiment was that they asked some subjects whether to push Chip Ellsworth III to save members of the Harlem Jazz Orchestra, but asked others whether to push Tyrone Patone to save members of the New York Philharmonic. Subjects were classed (based on a questionnaire) as either liberal or conservative. All participants agreed (after the experiment) that the answer to the moral dilemma should not be based on race.

Due to the names of the people who could be pushed, and the musical groups that could be saved, this was clearly a question about race. Liberals in the USA have strong explicit attitudes in support of minority groups, and these affected their answers. Liberals were more likely to endorse pushing Chip than Tyrone (conservatives were even-handed).

The participants were then given the alternative scenario, so those who had been asked whether they would push Chip were now asked whether they would push Tyrone and vice versa. Because the volunteers had already given a decision on whether to push the other fellow, any difference in their answer would demonstrate to an onlooker, and to participants themselves, that race had affected their answers. So they answered the second question in the same way that they'd answered the first question: endorsing pushing Chip if they had endorsed pushing Tyrone, and giving Tyrone a shove if they would have pushed Chip. Because liberals were initially more likely to agree to push Chip than Tyrone, it meant that the group of liberals who were asked about Tyrone as a second question were more likely to push him than those who were asked about Chip as a follow-up question. They ended up giving exactly the opposite answers to what they would have done if they'd been given the questions in the reverse order.

This example of motivated reasoning shows that we are able to produce responses and reasoning apparently in line with our consciously held and describable values. In the first question, liberals managed their answers in line with their political beliefs to avoid being racist. In the absence of a baseline, they over-compensated to demonstrate their conscious attitudes and were less likely to agree to pushing Tyrone than they would otherwise be. When answering the second question they had a baseline and were able to apply their egalitarian principles.

Without the controlled experiment, there would have been no way for observers, or consciousness, to know that participants' answers were caused by stereotypes. This experiment shows subjects actively managing how they are perceived, and acting in a manner that is consistent with particular views; and these views are consciously held, as we would expect them to be if the primary role of consciousness is to create a model based on external perceptions and to give advice based on that model about the social consequences of our behaviour.

Doing things for reasons we understand can lead us astray.

Researchers asked students to evaluate five posters and then choose one to take home.[100] Before letting them choose, they asked half of the students to write down reasons why they liked or disliked each poster.

You might expect that the group who gave reasons for their choice would be happier with their selection. They'd put more thought into it. But in coming up with conscious reasons, what they'd really done was choose a poster that had positive aspects they were capable of explaining to someone else. They could defend liking it, and misinterpreted this as actually liking it. On the day of the experiment, both groups rated their chosen posters equally positively. But weeks later, when the experimenters contacted the students again, they found that the students who hadn't given reasons for being attracted to one poster or another preferred their pick and were more likely to have hung it on their wall.[101]

Asking consciousness how we will be perceived after we have done something is like asking a management consultant whether a factory will be profitable after we've built it.

We've seen that in many ways we infer the contents of our own mind in the way that other people infer the contents of our mind. But we can only infer what other people are thinking from what they have already done. An apparent difference between the model we build of ourselves and the model other people build of us is that we frequently know what we are going to do before we do it.[102]

This might seem to be a weakness in the theory we are building. If other people only infer our decision to act after we have acted, then surely that is how we should infer our own minds too? However, if the social model that leads to consciousness is to be useful, this asymmetry is necessary.

I'm sitting here trying to think and write. My neighbours are next door listening to dance music. Very loudly. I've decided that if they haven't finished partying in ten minutes I'm going to ask them to turn it down. But if conscious awareness is primarily for inferring mental states, how can I be aware of this decision before I've knocked on the door? Surely I should hear myself asking them to be quieter and then infer that I did so because the noise was getting on my nerves. But being aware of possible decisions before I've acted on them is a necessity if our internal model is to be of any use. I have to consider whether my neighbours will do as I ask or laugh at me and ramp up the volume. I have to work out what my hip brother-in-law, who is staying with me at the moment, will think of me if I act like a grumpy old man. I have to feed this knowledge back to the decision-making process so it has the chance to reconsider.

I decide that I'll use earplugs. Now I do some inferring. I conclude that I changed my mind because my brother-in-law would indeed think less of me if I went next door. But at this stage I might be very wrong.

The brain feeds decisions to my model and it feeds sensory data, but it never gives reasons for its decisions. If I'd been subliminally primed with the concept 'aggression' I would have been more likely to complain. But I wouldn't have known that I'd been primed. I'd have been forced to conclude that the noise was just too loud and I had to do something about it.

If I only consciously knew what I might do after I'd done it, my ability to calculate other people's likely responses would be useless. Asking a consultant what you should do once you've made your decision isn't a good use of money, and inferring what other people will think of your actions only after you've performed them isn't a good use of brain power.

Our eyes are on the front of our head,
which makes looking at ourselves difficult.

Another apparent difference between the way we model
ourselves in consciousness and the way that other people model
us is the types of information we have access to. I can build
my model of you by looking at what you do, hearing what you
hear, smelling what you smell. But I can't taste what you taste
or feel what you feel. In using these senses to build your
conscious model of yourself you are using things that I cannot
possibly be using. Yet for us to build a model that reflects what
other people will infer about us, this asymmetry of information
is necessary due to the design of our senses.

Sight is our most important social sense,[103] and our eyes are
designed for looking at other people (and things) rather than
ourselves. To capture the information that other people are
receiving about us, we must use other senses to compensate.

Imagine that the two of us are sitting in a park. I am looking
at you and you are looking at me. Some children are playing
behind us, and one of them kicks a ball so that it hits me on
the back of the head and rolls away. I jump up and spin around.
You have seen the ball hit me and know why I am doing what
I am doing. If my self-model didn't receive information from
my nervous system, what could I conclude? Perhaps I apologise
for my sudden urge to stretch my legs or the desire to dance
(having inferred that you think I'm mad). Until the children
apologise to me or run away with the ball, I have no idea what

they are thinking, because I have no way of inferring what they should think I might be thinking. The only way for me to truly infer what you and they are thinking about me is to get some information in ways that you don't. And if you were looking away when the ball hit the back of my head I can guide you to the right answer by saying 'Ouch!' and, once I've seen the ball, passing some comment on what I think of careless children.

So we've found another way in which the tools we use to infer our own mind are different to those we use to infer other people's minds. At first glance, these differences seem to be problems for our social theory of consciousness: if we want to work out what other people are thinking we are thinking, surely we should infer what we are thinking in exactly the way that they make their inferences. However, this asymmetry doesn't make us less able to work out what other people are thinking about us; it paradoxically makes us better at it.

We feel our pain in the way that others see
our pain.

We need to feel pain directly to work out what other people
are thinking about us, and to explain our behaviour to them.
Yet our bias for modelling ourselves in the way that other people
can model us is so strong that even with pain, that apparently
most internal of sensations, we still use the type of information
accessible to other people to moderate how much we think we
hurt.

We use what they can see. Researchers mildly hurt participants'
hands while showing them a video clip on a screen positioned
between their eyes and their hand.[104] When the video clip was of
a hand with a needle puncturing the skin, the participants claimed
to hurt more than when the video was of a hand being prodded
with a cotton bud.

We also use cues that other people might use to guess how
much we are about to be hurt. People report a laser pulse to
be more or less painful when they are led to expect it to be more
or less painful.[105] We need pain information in ways that aren't
accessible to other people, but our experience of pain is moder-
ated by what our brain knows other people can observe.

We touch with our eyes, not just with our hands.

There are other circumstances where it is impractical to model ourselves as others model us, by relying only on the information that they have access to. It would be wasteful for me to watch every movement or gesture I make. Yet when I spill water from my glass or cross my fingers behind my back it is preferable that my model of myself knows about it before your reaction to what I have done[106] gives me that information. So even though you don't have direct access to feedback from the movements of my muscles, that feedback is consciously accessible to me: even without looking down, I can tell when I have overturned my glass of water. As with pain, it is useful to me in building a model of myself as you will build a model of me to receive some information in a way that you don't.

But again, even though we get these motor response signals, and it is clear why such signals are useful for constructing a model of ourselves, we still supplement them with externally observable cues to infer what we are doing.

The classic experiments showing this involve subjects drawing lines.[107] Using mirrors or computer screens, experimenters manipulate the line that subjects see themselves drawing. In order to draw what they see as a straight vertical line, participants actually have to draw a line that deviates to one side. When the deviation between what participants see and what they are drawing is very large (above about fourteen degrees), subjects are aware that the line they are drawing deviates from the image that they observe on the screen.[108] However, with smaller deviations, subjects correct the trajectory of their movements to produce the desired line on the screen without being aware that they are doing so. The brain, which controls the hand, knows that it is having to draw a curved line to one side, and does so, but it doesn't tell consciousness. Consciousness infers from what it is seeing that the hand is moving vertically.[109]

Our brains use motor feedback and visual feedback to adjust our actions. But, unless the two are very different, the visual feedback, which is more easily available to outside observers, dominates our perception of what we are doing.

We know things other people do not know,
which helps us to know what they will do.

A third asymmetry between our conscious experience and the way that other people model us is our memory. We know things they don't. But knowing that we know something that other people do not, and knowing that they do not know that we know it, can be highly useful in predicting what they will predict about us.

For example, imagine that I return to the changing rooms after a swim. I know that my clothes are in locker 87. But there is a man at the door of that locker. To everyone else in the changing rooms, it would seem that he has forgotten his code for he is rapidly trying different numbers.

When the man at the locker door sees my red face, he will probably infer that I am cross – or afraid. He may even be able to infer that my stuff is in locker 87. If I approach him, his response will depend on how he models me. Am I stronger than him, do I look like I will fight, can he convince me that he's just forgotten which locker is his?

But my knowledge that my locker is 87 gives me the upper hand. I can work to prevent him from making the inferences that would help him by walking straight past the locker to my heavily built friend. I can change the contents of my friend's mind by telling him what I know, and before this I must do some inferring myself: will my friend help me, why will my friend think I am approaching him? Many of these inferences can best be predicted by modelling myself in the way that my friend will. My fear and anger can be read from my face, body and tone. I have a good track record of not making this sort of joke. My thin arms are all too visible with a towel wrapped around my waist.

But the central piece of information – that my clothes are in locker 87 – is private. Without this piece of information, I could not make the decision to walk past the man trying to get into the locker. I could not tell my friend. These decisions rely on my social inferences about other people (and my inference of what they will infer about me), but for me to make these inferences I need to put the private information into the modelling process. My model needs information that other people don't have in order to accurately predict what they will do. Therefore, I should be conscious of things other people cannot possibly know, even though the model that produces consciousness is for predicting other people's responses to my actions.[110]

A lamp doesn't need to know why it shines light when its switch is flicked. We don't need to know why we do what we do when we do it either.

A lamp can be thought of as a simple decision-making device. When I flick the switch, it takes input from different sources. Am I plugged in? Is my filament intact? Is the fuse in place? If the answer to all these is yes, it 'decides' to emit light. The lamp doesn't need to know or understand anything about electricity or photons. Yet it works.

But a model of how a lamp works is of interest to physicists, engineers, and writers with a lamp that doesn't work. They want to predict the behaviour of the lamp and to manipulate it. So they model it abstractly. Physicists can model light as a wave and that predicts a lot. They can model a beam of light as a stream of particles and that explains other things. Engineers can model the lamp as a circuit with electricity pouring around the wires, and use this to work out how large the fuse should be. My model is simpler and helps me to get it to work.

To operate, the lamp doesn't need to understand any of these things. Similarly, the decision-making part(s) of the brain are complicated neuronal switches which don't need to understand anything: they have to respond to information not understand it. When I touch something hot it's important that signals are sent around my body that cause me to pull my hand away, but none of the circuits sending these signals need know that they are operating a hand, that the hand is hot or that if they don't work the hand will be damaged, any more than the lamp needs to know that if it doesn't shine light I won't be able to keep writing. It's only because we want to predict and manipulate other people that we have an abstract model of them with goals, intentions, emotions and thoughts.

## The model, not the construction of the model, is consciousness.

The states that we infer in our model of ourselves are what we call consciousness. My model is asked: 'What can I see?' and the answer is my conscious experience of vision. How am I feeling? I'm irritable. That is my conscious experience of feeling. Why did I step on your toe? Because I'm irritable and the reader jostled me. That is my conscious experience of reasoning.

This type of information is what our model of ourselves uses, and there's no reason for it to exist in any other process in the brain. The rest of our brain doesn't use such models. It acts like the lamp or my computer. It responds to signals and it sends out other signals of its own. There aren't any modelling states to be conscious of.

We're not even conscious of how the model gets its knowledge of the states. How did my model decide that I was irritable? It might be that it took into account my heart rate. It might be that the gum I'm chewing had formed my face into a frown at the time I asked it how I was feeling. It might be that my blood sugars are low because I've not eaten since breakfast. These are conceivable answers. We've seen that our conscious experience of our emotions are formed by just such cues. But my model doesn't tell me how it really decided. It can't. This information is turned into the states in our model, but the model has no reason to retain the information on how we got these states.

I can ask the model. It might answer that I'm grumpy because

I argued with my wife this morning. It might answer that I'm prickly because I've not eaten since breakfast. These may or may not have anything to do with why my model is really telling me I'm irritable. But they are my conscious experience of why I'm irritable.

## If we're not in control of our thoughts, must somebody else be?

It's odd that we sometimes create minds for ball bearings, cars and computers. But this isn't the limit of our mind-creating capacity. We can also invent minds that interfere with our own mind when it doesn't do what we want it to do.

Most people believe that their minds are one thing they can always control. Roman Catholics even confess each week that they have sinned in their thoughts as well as in what they have done and failed to do. But it can be very difficult to exert power over your thoughts. Try *not* to think of a car for a few minutes. If you're at all like me, you'll probably have thought about more different types of car in that time than you ever have before, and the harder you tried to suppress the images the more of them you'll have thought of.

But if you didn't willingly think of all those cars, who made you? You are forced to blame it on yourself, or perhaps on me for asking you to try the exercise. But scientists at Harvard gave volunteers the chance to blame it on something else.[111] Their participants listened to garbled noises recorded in the cafeteria, but were told that the noises in fact contained subliminal messages. The researchers asked half of the volunteers to avoid thinking of cars while writing down their thoughts on paper. They told the others to deliberately think about cars. Afterwards, they asked the participants how much they thought the hidden messages had influenced their thoughts. Those who had been trying unsuccessfully not to think of Fords, Toyotas and Porsches were more likely to say that these thoughts came from the recording than those who wanted to think of them.

We readily infer minds in all sorts of things we can't control. Our ancestors had gods of the wind, the seasons, the sea. And when we can't control our own mind, we're happy to invent another one that can control it.

If we had the type of consciousness we imagine that we have it would be useless, and so would we.


Our conscious experience is the output of a deeply flawed model. It's a bit embarrassing, frankly. So why don't we have a better one? When we model other people, we have obvious limitations. But we could do better with ourselves. Our self-model could be given direct access to the decision maker. Instead of guessing why I stood on your toe, or smiled at a cartoon, my brain could just tell me. If you were designing a mind, perhaps this is what you would start by doing. But I think that there are at least two reasons why you would quickly scrap your design and return to the flawed model of ourselves we actually have.

The first is a practical reason. There may be no central decision maker in the brain, and even if there is, the way it works and the information in it may not be very useful to the model. Think back to our basic robot with light sensors on the front and back and two motors independently driving sets of wheels. As we designed it, there was no central decision maker which we could give a perfect consciousness to.[112]

There's a second reason you'd fail your mind-designing course.

Your examiners would ask what the point of your self-model was. Because if your creature's mind had direct access to its own decision maker, its mind couldn't be helping your creation to work out what other creatures were thinking, because they don't have access to your creation's decision maker. For the mind to be of any use in understanding and predicting other robots' behaviour, it has to be built in the way that the other creatures are building their models of your robot's mind. So if your creation is to have a complicated social life you'd have to go away and design something else to help your robot navigate the social world.

If we had a perfect consciousness, we wouldn't be able to tell anyone about it.

The consciousness we are able to study isn't the final decision maker in the brain, it isn't the meeting place of all our thoughts and senses, and it isn't the place we set our overarching goals. But consciousness is so powerful that perhaps something like consciousness could be good for these things. We could have a second consciousness. The perfect model that we imagine we have. It could integrate information from across the brain, make our decisions and plan for the future.

As far as we know, humans only have one consciousness. But why couldn't we have two? One makes guesses that are helpful socially. The second is accurate. It's the consciousness we'd like to have.

Let's imagine that we do indeed have both of them. I'm here writing about my conscious experience. Am I writing about the social model or am I writing about the perfect consciousness that makes final decisions and is needed for integrating information?

When we write or talk we're doing something fundamentally social. When you tell me something, you're putting an idea from your head into mine. I might even change my behaviour as a result. So my brain has to ask questions. Why are you telling me this? How do you know? In turn, what you say has to reflect this. What will I infer about you from what you say? How will I react?

The tool we have for working out the answers to these questions is our social model. So when we communicate, it has to be by reference to the first consciousness. It is this that makes the types of inferences that you will when you hear me. We wouldn't expect this social model to be connected to the imagined perfect consciousness for the same reason it shouldn't ordinarily have access to the decision maker(s) in the brain: having real information about why we make decisions could distort the mistaken inferences that we need to have.

So hypothetically we could have the type of consciousness we imagine we do. But it wouldn't be the one that we're referring to when we talk about consciousness, and the one we do talk of won't know about it.

Animals can behave socially without knowing anything about minds.

When I see a dog with a wagging tail, I imagine that I know the dog is pleased to see me. As I like dogs, I might go and give him a stroke, and will be reasonably confident that he's not going to bite me. But dogs could use these cues without any model of their own or other dogs' mental states. They could work to rules.

If they come across another dog that is wagging its tail, they run up to them and give them a sniff. If the dog is growling and bigger than them, they run back to their master. They don't need to follow every step of the reasoning: that the dog is wagging his tail so he's happy to see me (the mental state); he's happy to see me, so he won't bite me if I give him a sniff (a conclusion drawn from the inferred mental state). Without any understanding of mental states it is possible to behave in a rudimentary (though far less flexible) socially adapted way.

We are not aware of peristalsis because our digestion is a boring subject for our friends.

Our body has to do lots of complicated things, but only a few of them are socially interesting. In the ordinary course of inter-action, your cells go on dividing, your digestive juices go on digesting and your pupils dilate or don't without having any impact on those around you. In normal situations, we do not try to predict other people's pupillary expansion and, as it usually works well, it is not useful to do so. As other people are not modelling these things for us, we do not need to model them in ourselves to understand other people's model of us. They are unconscious.

It is speech and the movements of our skeletal muscles that are interesting to other people. It is through these that we communicate; initiate sex; hunt, steal or share food; fight; run away; defecate in the drinking water or pull a tick from some-body else's back. So it is the movements of these, and the intentions to move them, that we are sometimes conscious of.[113]

Once we've mastered a skill it is the decision to use this skill rather than the mechanical details that are interesting.

As we learn a new motor skill, many neurological changes occur.[114] In parallel with gaining proficiency, practised motor skills become automatic.[115] This is because we only model socially relevant behaviour. When we first learn a motor skill, the mechanical details of our actions are socially relevant, but once we have mastered the skill it is our decision to deploy our abilities that is socially relevant.

Consider a learner driver. They will receive a stream of instructions which will be based on what the instructor thinks the learner knows and is thinking. 'Check your mirror before you signal.' 'Lift the clutch gently.' 'Don't be nervous when you pull out.'

For an experienced driver, the socially relevant decision is that he has decided to back the car out of the garage. The details of clutch control, checking mirrors, lifting the hand-brake have ceased to be of interest to other people and are done automatically, without reference to their social model. Because consciousness is the result of our social model of ourselves, we are preferentially conscious of actions that are socially relevant, and we don't waste conscious resources on skills that have ceased to be so.

We are aware of conflicts because they are interesting.

In normal circumstances you will not pay any attention to my breathing. It is of no more social interest than my pupillary reflex. So I breathe without noticing I am doing so. However, if we go shell-hunting and I have to hold my breath to swim under the water, my breathing becomes socially interesting. Will I hold my breath for long enough to reach the conch that we have seen?

I have a conflict to solve between getting the shell and surfacing where breathing is easier. My prediction of what you will think of me if I surface, and what you will do given what you think of me, will affect how hard I try. If I surface will you conclude that I tried my hardest or that I gave up easily? If I fail will you dive down to get the shell, and will you give it to me afterwards? If I am a poor shell-hunter with no stamina will you come shell-hunting with me again? Social considerations feed into the best decision of how much effort I should put into getting the shell (though as we cannot asphyxiate ourselves by holding our breath, it does not have the ultimate say), and therefore holding our breath, unlike normal breathing, is something that we are consciously aware of.[116]

We hear our name in a crowded room
because we are the most interesting thing
to ourselves.

At a cocktail party, we filter out the hubbub of conversations around us and focus on what the person opposite is telling us. But then, suddenly, we hear our name: we are being talked about behind us. We hear all the rumours that are being spread about us, and blush with shame.

It turns out that our ears are picking up, and our brains processing, lots of conversations. But our conscious brains are expensive tools with limited capacity. So our unconscious brains don't overload them with all the information they're processing behind the scenes. They send the information that consciousness can most usefully opine on: socially relevant information. Usually that is what the person talking to us is saying, but when that's not the case the unconscious brain knows enough about what is socially interesting to switch our attention.[117] When somebody says our name we need to understand the implications of what they're saying and how they will respond if we turn around and correct the terrible rumours they're spreading. For that we need our social models, our conscious brains, and that is why we hear our name in a crowded room.

Your big brain is the reason I have a big
brain.

The hardest and most important thing humans can do isn't
mathematics, philosophy, engineering or even science. It's
dealing with other people. We're more complicated than algebra,
deeper than metaphysics and less predictable than earthquakes.
Everything we want we get through other people.

Primates who live in bigger groups have bigger brains,[118] and
humans have more intricate, flexible social relationships than
any other animal. We are able to live in cities, transact with
people we have never before met, and form teams to undertake
abstract projects that have never been done before. Our use of
language enables us to talk about people who are not here,
describe the nuances of feeling and motivation, exchange complicated ideas, plan sophisticated projects that will take years or
generations to execute, and not least deceive others in ways that
no other animal can. To do all this, and work out what people
really want when they tell us something, takes brain power, and
it's competitive.

If you're better at predicting people's behaviour and influencing them than I am, you will get the high-status job, nab the
guy or gal and outwit me. I need a big brain just to understand
you.

Getting ourselves right is harder – and less important – than getting other people right.

The gap between self-perception and how people appear to others is the source of much humour, whether it's Ricky Gervais's character in *The Office*, John Cleese's Basil Fawlty, Larry David in *Curb Your Enthusiasm*, Charles Pooter in *The Diary of a Nobody*, or Bottom in *A Midsummer Night's Dream*. But it's hard for us to see ourselves as others see us, even though other people's perception of us is often more accurate.

We're designed for inferring other people's minds, and inferring what other people are thinking about us is a secondary adaptation. It's not a surprise it doesn't work as well. Worse still, we're stuck with one consciousness and have to adjust from this one model to estimate how hundreds of people see us. My wife might think my new leather jacket is gorgeous, so I go out thinking I look great. Unless they tell me, how do I know most people think I look a twit in it?

Even when we tell people what we're thinking, we can fail to understand what they will learn about us. When we tell somebody something negative about ourselves, we expect them to like us less for it. This might be true when we tell our partner, who already knows us well: the one new thing that they have learnt is the negative thing we have told them. But for people who aren't already intimate with us, they have learnt a second thing: that we are honest and open. This second piece of information may outweigh the content of our negative disclosure and (unless we have admitted something truly dreadful) they may like us more for it. Indeed, in at least one experiment,[119] participants liked somebody who opened up about their weaknesses as much as somebody who told them something attractive about themselves.

We all know somebody who seems incapable of seeing himself or herself in the way that other people see them. Some managers seem particularly susceptible to this gap, whether it's because they don't care what we think of them, they needed a thick skin to get where they are, or we just have a particularly warped view of them ourselves.[120] So next time your boss is spouting grandiose nonsense remember that this is a fine comic moment and resist the temptation to tell him or her that you'd like them far more if they opened up about their uncertainties.

Minds are hard to study because they are good at their job.

The job of a social psychologist is to understand how we work: what causes us to do, say, believe or think one thing rather than another. But over thousands of generations, humans have had to answer the same questions every day. If we couldn't predict what other people will do, we couldn't live the lives we do.

The way scientists usually gain knowledge is to start with a bad model. They then find out the points at which the model breaks down and invent a better one that predicts more things more accurately. So we used to have a model of atoms as solid, indivisible balls, then we had a model of atoms as positively charged balls with negative electrons scattered inside it, then we had a model of atoms as small positively charged nuclei with electrons orbiting them and now physicists have moved on from this. Each model explained most of what we knew at the time and was better than the preceding one.

But for human behaviour, scientists were in a different position. We have an inbuilt, brilliant model for predicting what we and other people will do. It isn't right, but it is very, very good. The hypothesis that minds exist and do broadly what we experience them to do made better predictions than anything scientists could invent.

Almost all of the experiments in this book were conducted long after the structure of DNA was discovered, man walked on the moon and the atom was split. Because our inbuilt model is so good it has taken a long time to find the places where the model breaks down – and so discard it in the way that we discarded failed models of atoms. The tremendous power of our minds is what has kept their workings hidden.

Minds are hard to study because we have them.

This new knowledge makes me uneasy. It is hard to accept that my conscious brain doesn't do what I experience it doing. That my unconscious sets my goals, initiates my actions, decides what I should be aware of and chooses what I do. It is still less pleasant to know that my conscious mind is the result of a flawed model designed to understand what *other* people are thinking.

In the past, scientific advances have upturned our views of the world and who we are. Quantum mechanics is strange because its explanation that the world is made of a hard-to-define swirl of probabilities doesn't accord with our experience. The findings of Darwin and Copernicus revolutionised how we saw our place in the world. But there has never been a finding as unsettling as this: our experience of experience isn't what we thought it was.

Consciousness is to the brain what a PR
agent is to a company.

When a company builds a factory, avoids or pays taxes, or expands in a new market it needs to know what the public thinks of it, what the public will do in response and what the company can do to change that response. To understand this, they might hire a public relations expert. The ideal PR agent should not cloud their judgment with knowledge of how the company views itself. Instead the agent should read the press, talk to people, and use what they know of human nature to understand how the public will view the company.

The agent doesn't need to know how profitable a project is or how much management cares about it. She doesn't need to know why management is thinking of doing what it is thinking of doing; her job is to figure out what the public will perceive the reasons to be. Similarly, management, which is busy enough already, doesn't need to know how the agent formed their opinions, which newspapers they read or who they spoke to. Once the PR agent has reported, it is management's responsibility to weigh the agent's advice against the potential profits and decide what to do. The agent doesn't make decisions, she just advises on her specialist subject. In the same way, our conscious brains don't need to know all the factors that actually go into a decision in order to work out how other people will infer what led to the decision. They don't need to report back what information they used to work out what other people would think of us, and it is the unconscious brain which ultimately decides whether to follow the advice of the conscious brain or do something else.

## Consciousness is for understanding other people, not ourselves.

In this book, we've presented a social theory of consciousness. Consciousness arises from a model of ourselves as other people will perceive us. So how did we get to such a theory? What were the clues that led us here, and what does it help us to explain that we couldn't explain without it?

The most obvious trail of evidence was in Part Three. We infer what we're thinking, feeling, wanting in much the same way as other people infer such drives in us. We rely on our expressions, posture, the situation and our observations of our actions rather than gaining conscious knowledge directly from whatever processes in our own brains actually determine our actions. If the point of consciousness is to understand other people, this is what we would expect. But this isn't sufficient to prove our theory, and our theory does more than this.

If this was all the evidence we had, we might conclude that consciousness was an accidental by-product of the device we have to infer other people's minds.[121] We have the tools to model others and a rogue bit of grey matter turns the tools in on ourselves, thus giving us consciousness. If this were true, consciousness would be pointless, a bit like male nipples.

But consciousness does more than this. We have additional tools to form a model of ourselves, and we use them in a different way. We use sensations that we don't have access to when forming judgements about other people, such as pain and motor feedback. We are often aware of what we will do before we do it, even when it would be impossible for somebody else to guess what we will do. We use private information that other people couldn't possibly have, such as the number of our locker.

If consciousness started out as a misuse of our tools for inferring other people's minds, it has changed a lot since then in very complicated ways. This suggests that consciousness as we now have it has evolved. The non-trivial way in which we infer our own minds suggests that there was selective pressure for it to become better at doing something: it had a purpose. Our ancestors who had consciousness that was more like our own did better than those who didn't in some way.

I propose that the thing they did better than other people was predicting the behaviour of others and manipulating them. They were better able to work out what other people would work out about them and so changed their own behaviour such that other people's behaviour would be more advantageous to them. This fits in well with other things we know about primate evolution: the driver of their large brains is social. It also fits with one thing we know for certain about consciousness: we can talk about it. Indeed this has been our working definition of what consciousness is: if we can't report seeing the flash or connect the wobbly bridge with our romantic decisions then it is because it is our unconscious alone doing the work. The fact we can and do talk about what we consciously experience opens it up to natural selection, and this selection is social: it is other people's decision to date us or punch us after hearing what we say, which determines whether we contribute genes to the next generation.

175

It is plausible that social pressures led to the asymmetries between the way we infer our own mind and the way we infer others'. It's also possible to argue that these asymmetries – the use of private information, the use of senses such as touch and the fact that we are sometimes aware of what we will do before we do it – are useful if consciousness is for working out what others will infer from what we do. But we also have direct evidence.

The experiments with the poor / rich girl called Hannah and the choice to bump off Chip or Tyrone provide it. In these experiments, participants acted in ways such that an outside observer would infer their consciously accessible attitudes from their behaviour. When they made a decision in circumstances where it would be difficult for an outside observer to infer what led to that decision, they went with their implicit attitudes: they were prejudiced. (As they weren't able to infer the causes of their behaviour either, they were unaware that they were behaving in a prejudiced manner.) But when they were able to work out that their decision could be attributed to a socially unacceptable motivation they made different decisions.

We've also found other supporting evidence for our posited social role of consciousness. If the role of consciousness is to help us analyse socially relevant information, then we might expect the brain to feed such information to it more readily than other information, and this is what we found. We infer a decision to breathe only when somebody else might care about that decision if they were observing us. Learned actions cease to be conscious when they're no longer socially interesting. We notice somebody else's voice in a crowded room when they say our name. Our unconscious must be registering and processing the information all the time, but it is only fed into consciousness when it is socially relevant.

An important difference between the social theory of consciousness we've explored[122] and many other theories[123] is its role in making decisions. Before experiments such as those described in this book were conducted, it might have seemed obvious what consciousness did, and many more recent theories try to salvage something from the wreckage of this obvious theory. We experience making decisions. Consciousness also has access to a lot of information: we experience sensations from our five senses and we know a great deal about what we will do, what we're contemplating doing and apparently know what we want. If consciousness doesn't make decisions, why does it have access to all of these things? Isn't the most natural explanation the one that says we have consciousness to combine many of the other things the brain is doing in one place, tie them together, and make a decision that weighs all the information and desires appropriately?[124] [125]

I'd argue that we have all this information because it helps us make better predictions about other people, and we note that there's lots of information the brain uses to make non-socially relevant decisions (such as how much to dilate our eyes, how far apart to extend our fingers when picking something up, or what chemicals to release into our bloodstream) which we don't have conscious access to.[126] I'd also argue that it is natural that we experience making conscious decisions because that is a major role of consciousness: working out why other people will believe we made a particular decision. It is also true that consciousness contributes to our decision making. If it didn't, it would be useless.

But our appetite contributes to our decision to eat, and what we see contributes to what we do. We wouldn't have either eyes or appetite if they didn't contribute to our decisions, yet it doesn't make sense to talk of either as being a decision maker. In the same way, the model of ourselves from which consciousness arises gives advice that leads to decisions, but doesn't make decisions itself.

If consciousness was a final decision maker, it would be very hard to explain why we are only aware of a subset of the information that is used to make the decisions we are aware of and also why we are so often mistaken about why we made a particular decision. Why do we think we know why we chose the stockings on the right of the display? Why do we think we know why we love someone? In the first parts of the book, we saw lots of examples in which subjects made a decision for reasons they were unaware of and yet still believed that they knew why they did what they did.

Perhaps, you could argue, consciousness makes a particular type of decision or integrates certain types of information. In this way, we would allow for experiments showing our romantic choices are unconscious and for other experiments showing that we can move our fingers without a conscious decision. According to this argument, consciousness does less than we imagine, but it does the sort of thing we imagine.

But there are powerful objections to this. Why are we mistaken about which decisions are conscious and why do we go to the trouble of combining incorrect information to create plausible explanations for why we consciously chose to do what we didn't consciously choose to do? Neither of these seem to further the ends of a conscious decision maker, and both seem to require a great deal of expensive brainpower to operate.

If we found a type of decision in which consciousness *was*

the final decider, say the decision to twiddle our toes, wouldn't it be far more efficient if consciousness focussed on whether or not we twiddle our toes rather than expending energy on things it demonstrably doesn't do, such as whether to fall in love or whether to be polite to an experimenter? Why create all these confabulations which convince us we made a conscious decision when we didn't? If consciousness was an aware decision maker, the least we could expect of it would be that it was aware of which decisions it was taking.

Finally, theories that propose that consciousness is needed for making some class of decisions have difficulty explaining the consciousness of consciousness. Simple animals make decisions that require the weighing of information from different senses and the balancing of drives, such as choosing whether to forage or stay in the safety of shelter. We don't necessarily infer that they (or indeed lamps) require consciousness to do so. Humans also combine information unconsciously (for instance in the McGurk effect, where we combine sight and sound). It is not clear why a decision maker should be *aware*. What is it that is so special about whatever type of decision consciousness might make that requires sentience for us to do it? Why are we aware of the vision we are aware of, but not the subliminal flashes which are processed by the brain and change our behaviour?

Our social theory of consciousness does offer an explanation. The abstract states of emotions, desires, field of vision etc., which perhaps only exist in our self-model, are naturally experienced. We do not think that there is a need to presume a gap between having these states and being conscious of them. They are our experience.

Our theory also offers an elegant explanation of why we only now know what consciousness is for. Consciousness is designed for predicting and explaining our behaviour, and is good at it. So the belief that we make conscious decisions for the reasons we are aware of is usually a good way to understand human behaviour, even if it is wrong.

PART FIVE

Consciousness is only one of many
advisers in the brain, and it can be made
more or less influential

Consciousness might be used for other things besides modelling ourselves, in the way that legs can be used for football, fingers for typing and disgust for morality.

Consciousness is an output from a system in the brain which has as its primary role the inferring of mental states. But it doesn't follow that this is all it does. When we think of hard, conscious thought, we think of maths, philosophy and logical reasoning.[127] This could be an accident. It might be that we're consciously aware of these things because we need to be able to talk about them; we need to discuss our conclusions and convince other people. Or it could be that consciousness has evolved a secondary role.

The kit for inferring mental states is tremendously powerful. To infer minds we have to draw on varied sources of information and sensibly combine them. We have to deal with abstract concepts and logically draw conclusions about other people. These tools might be useful elsewhere.

There are lots of examples in psychology[128] of methods the brain has developed for one purpose being re-used for something else rather than reinvented from scratch. We saw an example earlier: the brain uses the same tools to form an aversion to dirty food and other contaminants as it does to disgusting moral actions rather than inventing a new set of tools to do a similar job. It might be that the tools we have to infer minds have been co-opted to do logical reasoning for us, and a side-effect is that we are conscious of the process. If asked why humans have legs, it is reasonable to answer that we have them to move around.

But this doesn't stop us from using them to kick a football (or person), dance or balance a book on them. In the same way, the main role of the model that leads to consciousness is a social one, but it doesn't necessarily follow that we don't use the tools of consciousness for logical reasoning, philosophy and so on.

Conversely, legs are not the only body part that we need to run, as we discover if we try to run with our arms folded. Without legs, it is also possible (though far harder) to move from one place to another. Just as it is possible to move around without legs, there are also unconscious processes that modify our interactions with other people.[129]

Consciousness isn't the only tool we have for predicting what other people will do, and the tools of consciousness have probably been co-opted into other roles. But neither of these detract from our claim that the main purpose of consciousness is in modelling ourselves socially, and that this was the likely driver of its development.

Consciousness is just one adviser in the brain, and it isn't the strongest one.

Understanding self-control might be one of the most important practical things that psychologists can do. People with more of it are healthier, get better grades, have happier romantic relationships, are less likely to commit crimes, and have more successful careers.[130]

Self-control is a battle between the advice that the self-model of consciousness gives to the brain and the advice of other advisers. These other processes in the brain are far older and have been influencing our behaviour long before we had a model of ourselves.

A dieter might decide that she will look more attractive if she cuts down on the cake. But her appetite is telling her brain to reach for another slice. A struggle in the brain ensues and she scoffs the last bit of cake.

Her conscious self-model then has the job of explaining her behaviour from her actions. It reasons that it was only one slice and she will start her diet tomorrow. As with all her actions, the reasoning behind the unconscious decision is inferred in consciousness and experienced as a conscious decision, even though the advice from the conscious self-model was that she shouldn't take the cake. This is the strange experience of a failure in willpower. As consciousness is built from her observed actions, she might in time infer that she's happy with her weight, that she lacks the willpower for a diet, or just that there are more important things in life. Then her self-model will stop advising the brain to avoid the cake and the diet will be over.

Willpower is more than a metaphor: it is possible to wear out our mental muscles.

When you think of somebody who has no willpower, you might describe them as weak willed or lacking mental strength. When they explain their failures, they might talk of struggles, being worn down and lacking mental stamina. In fact, this metaphor linking self-control with physical exertion is a very good one.

If willpower is a limited resource then it ought to get worn out. If I go for a swim before a trip to the gym, I'm not able to lift many weights. I've depleted my muscles. The same is true of our mental strength.

A research group in Ohio had fun showing this.[131] They asked some participants to spend six minutes not thinking about a white bear. This task is surprisingly difficult (try it yourself). It's the equivalent of not thinking about the beautiful weather outside while you're working. The more you try not to, the more you do.

After the volunteers had finished thinking or not thinking about polar bears plodding across the Arctic, Rupert the bear waving through the window, and snowy stuffed toys coming alive, the researchers gave them some anagrams to solve. Solving the anagrams was even more difficult: the experimenters had deliberately made them impossible. If we can exhaust our willpower, then people who have just tried valiantly to control their thoughts ought to have less stamina left and give up more quickly on the unsolvable anagrams than participants who had thought about whatever they wanted before the task. This is exactly what the researchers found.

Interestingly, making choices wears out the same mental muscles as exercising self-control. Volunteers who choose between alternative shampoos, T-shirts and socks are less able to hold their hands in cold water for long periods of time.[132] It shouldn't surprise us that supermarkets put the chocolate, wine and crisps at the end of the store. If we want to reduce our shopping bill, we should start at the back of the shop when we have plenty of energy to resist temptation and finish in the fruit and vegetable section.

If you want to get close to your partner, forget flowers, nice food and compliments: ask them to proofread an essay.

Proving that they have great stamina themselves, researchers have demonstrated the same effect with an array of different tasks to tire out subjects and measure their mental exhaustion.[133] They've had participants squeezing handles, holding their breath, avoiding smiling while watching a comedy, thinking about death, proofreading, and eating radishes instead of choco- late chip cookies. All of their results show the same thing: expending mental effort on one task reduces that available for a second bout of self-control.

An interesting experiment for amorous-minded readers demonstrated that sexual restraint can be exhausted in the same way.[134] Couples who'd only been dating a short time controlled their attention in a short video-watching task, during which the experimenters attempted to distract them. Afterwards they were left alone. The couples who were more depleted expressed more 'physical intimacy' than those who hadn't done the attention-control task.

Exercise strengthens your mental muscles as well as your physical muscles.

To improve your physical fitness, you train. If you want to build muscles you lift weights. If you want stamina you swim, cycle or run. Exercise temporarily tires our muscles, but in the long term it strengthens them. You can strengthen your mental muscles in the same way.

Keeping to a physical exercise regime is in itself a workout for our self-restraint. In the long run we are happier if we exercise, but before any session the alternatives are more appealing: reading, watching a film or going for a drink with our friends are all more pleasurable for most of us. Megan Oaten and Ken Cheng thought that enrolling on an exercise programme might be good for our minds as well as our bodies.[135]

Half of the participants in their study received a personal training regime which included aerobics and weight lifting. At the end of the two-month programme, the researchers tested the self-control of the volunteers by first depleting them (using the white bear exercise) and then attempting to distract them while the participants tried to keep track of moving black boxes on a computer screen. The participants who'd exercised did far better.

As well as improving on the researchers' artificial tests of self-control, participants also improved on useful measures. They reported studying more and watching less television, they spent less and they even claimed to wash their dishes instead of leaving them in the sink.[136]

# Drinking sugary drinks can enhance your willpower.

Athletic feats are such a good metaphor for self-control because willpower runs off the same juice as our thighs and biceps. The brain consumes a huge amount of energy. It may only be a little organ, weighing about a fiftieth of our total mass, but it uses a fifth of the body's calories.

Managing conflicts between what our conscious self-model is proposing and what other parts of the brain are proposing is a particularly hungry part of what our brains do. When we exercise self-control, our blood glucose levels drop. With less energy available, we are less able to exert willpower on subsequent tasks.

Choosing our battles is key to winning. Don't plan to write a difficult report, diet and give up smoking all at the same time.* But our physiological understanding of willpower also suggests a straightforward way to replenish it. Drink Lucozade. Just as an endurance athlete can be given a boost by sipping a glucose

---

*The latter two are particularly difficult. Nicotine causes cells to release glucose into the blood. When smokers give up, a side effect is that their blood glucose levels plummet. Without the energy needed to exercise willpower, they become irritable, have trouble concentrating, and find it difficult to avoid buying more cigarettes. There's some evidence that taking sugar tablets at the same time as NRT or bupropion can improve quitters' success.[137] Dieting also has the potential to reduce the blood sugar levels, making it particularly difficult to exert enough willpower to stick to the diet.

drink, if you're worn out by mental exertion, drinking sugary lemonade gives you back your stamina.[138] Unfortunately, this fix isn't much help to you if what you need willpower for is keeping to your diet.

If you believe you will win it's more likely to happen.

Some athletes speak as if belief rather than training is the key to sporting success. Michael Jordan: 'You have to expect things of yourself before you can do them.' Tiger Woods: 'My mind is my biggest asset. I expect to win every tournament I play.' In terms of exercising mental strength, there are also benefits to believing in yourself. Once consciousness has determined that you're likely to fail, it stops sending signals to the brain to do the socially preferred thing and instead uses its resources to explain why you've failed.

One group of researchers manipulated volunteers' perceptions of whether they had plenty of energy available or were depleted.[139] For the first task, participants searched through a dull document for certain combinations of letters. The scientists then convinced some of the students that this task had been tiring and others that it hadn't, telling them of (fictitious) previous research showing that the colour of the paper on which they were working would affect how weary they felt.

Afterwards, they measured how much effort the volunteers put into a second task: completing anagrams. The students who had been convinced that they had no reason to feel depleted got a second wind: they worked more than 75% longer than those who thought the first task had tired them out.

Giving people confidence that they have the resources to do something makes it easier for them. But sometimes we do the opposite. Cigarette packets carry the message: 'Smoking is highly addictive.' Promoting the belief that quitting smoking is hard to do may make it even more difficult. Dieters sometimes get together to talk about how much trouble they have avoiding their favourite snacks. Rather than helping each other, they might actually be undermining their success. If Michael Jordan had the mantra, 'Basketball's really hard, but I'm going to give it my best shot,' he might not have gained the nickname 'Air Jordan'.

Having a picture of your family on your desk might make you work harder, but you'll be rattier when you get home.

Most of us learn about self-control from our families. We're taught to eat Brussels sprouts, go to bed early and not hit our brothers. In later life, our families are a motivation to use self-control. We work hard, cut down on our drinking and avoid snapping at our bosses to make their lives better.

Thoughts of our family therefore increase our brain's reasons to use its limited resources: even when we don't realise we're thinking about our family. In one experiment, subjects sat a thirty-question maths exam at a computer.[140] While they focused on their mental multiplication, half of them saw names of members of their family flashed on the screen. As in other subliminal priming experiments, the flashes were too short for participants to notice consciously but long enough for the unconscious to process (about three hundredths of a second).

After the maths test, the experimenters asked participants to create as many words as possible from the letters *m, p, l, a,* and *e.* Subjects who had seen the names of family members worked harder at the task and came up with more words. Forcing yourself to sit still while you stare at the letters and think *lap, leap, map, lamp, maple, ape,* is a triumph of conscious will over the desire to leave the lab and drink a glass of *ale* with a *pal,* but the energy you spend on the task is affected by what your unconscious is thinking.

When I first started work, a senior manager gave me some

advice on how to get ahead in the business. One of the things he told me was never to become one of those workers who pinned a photo of their family next to their computer screen. 'What they're telling me,' he said, 'is that they'd rather be at home playing with their kids or hugging their wife than sitting here and making money for the firm. That might be how you feel, but never let your boss know that.' What this manager didn't understand was that the psychological presence of their families might have given his subordinates the strength to stay late crunching numbers and writing reports for him. The pictures may have motivated them to use up all their energy keeping their jobs, leaving them with less energy when they went home. His distaste for family snaps may have cost the company money, and improved the home life of his workers.

If we look after our brain it will allow us to do more of what we want to do.

Consciousness and conflict are intimately linked. The brain frequently has to weigh up and make decisions between competing impulses. Not all of these conflicts are evolutionarily new. Most animals have to decide between foraging for food and staying safe from predators; between conserving energy and hunting. Even fruit flies take bigger risks when they're hungry.[141] But humans are aware of these conflicts because they're socially interesting: other people want to predict what decision we will make.

Consciousness also contributes to a whole new type of conflict. We don't have an innate drive to sit in an office editing spread-sheets, to study for exams, to write books or to shave. We do these things because of the impact they will have on other people.[142] In humans, the way we best understand how other people will interpret our actions is through the social models that create consciousness. When we choose to work hard in the office in spite of being hungry or tired, we are creating a conflict between doing the socially preferable thing (as advised by our conscious brains) and following an impulse that existed before mammals did.

Managing these conflicts in our brain is energy intensive. When we are low on glucose, or don't use it effectively, it isn't the older impulses which lose out, it is the conscious adviser. For modern humans, the weighting our brains give to these older impulses is perhaps too high. We would achieve more in our food-rich, socially complicated lives if we studied more, worked harder and put more effort into cultivating relationships.[143] We can improve our self-control by managing our glucose levels.[144]

An extreme example of failing to do the socially desirable thing is criminality. A long-term study on released prisoners found that their physiological response to glucose was a strong predictor of future violence.[145] Improving diet in prisons reduces violence among inmates.[146]

One way to improve our self-control (and mood)[147] is to eat breakfast. Our glucose levels drop during the night and need replenishing. When schools gave free breakfasts to their pupils, students' attentiveness in classes improved.[148]

We should also get a good night's sleep before we have our breakfast. After a night deprived of sleep, volunteers did less well on an attention control task: their brains metabolised glucose less well.[149]

To win the battles in our brain, our conscious advisers need resources. Arming them with the energy they need, giving them social motivation in the form of family and supporters they rely on, training them through exercise, and avoiding picking too many fights at once will make them, and us, more successful.

A great actor doesn't act as the character would; he acts as the audience imagines the character would.

In the same way, our conscious brain isn't interested in how we actually are, but in how our audience will perceive us to be. The real us isn't visible to the audience. Other people can only interact with the characters we play and we take direction from a part of the brain that sits in the wings observing our performance.

Great novelists attempt to unveil the human mystery, but really they just examine the pattern on the veil.

Novels are about people and the way they behave. They are about dilemmas, whether it's that of a spy thriller in which fraught Oxbridge-types balance immoral acts with the greater good or that of a period romance in which the pressures of society oppose a love-match. They are about minds. But novelists are constrained in the same way that actors are: their characters have to behave in ways that we find believable. Characters in novels are more independent than humans really are, they're less influenced by others' unconscious mimicking, and they rarely misattribute their fear of crossing a wobbly bridge to sexual passion.[150]

However, the techniques that writers use to tell their stories can tell us how our brains work, even if the writers themselves don't know why they use the techniques they do. A difference between an enjoyable book and one that isn't is the way the author moves us from one process in our brain to another, evoking emotions on the way. This is especially true of those novels that we read not because we think they will be improving, or because we are tricked into believing the writer will tell us something profound, but because the author grips us.

Nobody wins a Nobel Prize for using clichéd metaphors, but our brain readily uses them and so do writers who want their work to be enjoyed rather than to win awards. Stormy arguments happen on stormy nights. Bad guys have deformities and strange habits to match their characters. Lady Macbeth endlessly tries to wash the blood from her hands.

Our understanding of consciousness also explains the writers' maxim, 'show, don't tell'. It's efficient for a novelist to tell you that Sally loves Mark. But as the conscious brain is designed to ask about motivations and infer minds it naturally asks why the writer is telling you this, how they know, whether they could be mistaken. When the novelist shows you that Sally has a picture of Mark by her bed, your conscious brain busies itself inferring Sally's mental states, rather than those of the author, for itself.

The experience of free will is our best guess at whether we will be blamed or commended for what we do.

Earlier in the book, we looked at the consequences of believing or not believing in free will. We're now in a position to look at the topic of free will from a different angle. I think that free will as most of us conceptualise it doesn't exist. But I don't think it matters. Free will is something we experience rather than have or don't have, and the experience is useful. We can experience doing something deliberately or accidentally, automatically or in a controlled way, of our own choosing or under coercion, and this tells us something about how other people may judge us.

Imagine I had a robot which did my housework. It breaks a plate. What I care about is whether it will break plates in the future. Was it a rare accident caused by an extremely slippery pasta sauce? Is the robot clumsy and better suited to making the bed? Or is the circuit that tells the robot to help its master fundamentally mangled, in which case I should melt the robot down?

These are similar to the evolutionary questions our ancestors had to ask. Who should you trust? Who is capable? How will they behave? It didn't matter whether their decisions were conscious or unconscious. But their best guess at whether you could be trusted was based on their model of your mind. Your best guess at their best guess was based on your model of their model of your mind. Your consciousness.

So the experience of conscious will and morality are linked. This link is what we call free will. That we now understand consciousness in a very different way doesn't change the questions we need to ask. Will this person steal again? How should I react? The experience of free will is the starting point for understanding how other people will judge us.

Knowing that you are trapped in an illusion doesn't help you to escape.

Your experience is that you make conscious decisions. You've now seen evidence that you don't. So by telling you all this have I robbed you of your conscious mind? Do you now feel like an automaton with a wonky model attached? Of course not. Knowing how an optical illusion works doesn't stop you from being tricked by it. At the end of this chapter, you will close the book, turn off the lamp and still have the overwhelming impression that these were conscious choices. But this doesn't mean that there aren't consequences of this new science.

I trust all that my physics teachers told me. But I still experience the sun rising in the morning and setting in the evening as if Copernicus had never been born. Yet Copernicus changed two things. He changed our view of our place in the world. Nobody now bases their theology on the Earth as the centre of things with the stars and planets paying it homage. He also changed how we manipulate the world. If you want to fly to the moon it is easier if you know where the moon will be when you get there. The great scientists conducting the experiments in this book have also done these two things.

# ACKNOWLEDGEMENTS

I'd like to thank all the researchers who thought of and carried out the experiments described in the book (and others that aren't in the book but which have been influential to my thinking). In and of themselves, I think that their experiments are interesting and useful. Taken together, I think they point towards a much bigger theory. Future generations of social psychologists may look back to the present as the time their subject became really interesting.

Thank you also to friends (Clare Devlin and Peter Smith) and family for looking at early versions of the manuscript.

My agent, James Wills, has been supportive of me and the book through several rewrites. My editor, Mark Booth, suggested a change to the structure of the book, which has improved it greatly.

My wife, Fiona, allowed me to write the book. Before we wed, she knew that I planned to leave my job as soon as I'd saved enough and research this book. She still married me, and while I often feel guilty for the things I gave the book rather than her, I am grateful that she encouraged me to do so.

My colleagues at Barclays Capital (as it then was) made my initial period of work far shorter than I had anticipated, and a lot more interesting. If banking and bankers had been what I expected, it would have been easy to leave the industry. As it was, they weren't and it wasn't. Adam Moses ranks as one of my best teachers: I was a different man after my time with him.

Some people are born lucky: they have wealth, beauty or some talent. I have been lucky to have great teachers and to recognise it. At school there were many. Two should be mentioned. Stuart Clarke's advice led directly to this book more than a decade after he gave it to me. A geography teacher I won't name (in case he's still in the profession) told me frankly that learning the geography syllabus was more or less a complete waste of my time. He told me to focus on the important subjects and those I cared for, and even recommended novels I should read rather than trudging through dreary homework assignments.

I've kept this selective attention to my studies throughout life – apologies to those supervisors who correctly discerned that I wasn't attending to certain courses of lectures as an undergraduate. Time to learn is the most valuable thing we are given. We shouldn't waste it. Learning things that are neither as interesting nor as useful as the things we could otherwise be doing is a perverse use of this gift.

Dr Bleloch and Dr Krivanek FRS probably don't know how much I appreciate what they gave me. Dr Taraskin and Professor Elliott hopefully do.

# NOTES

1. Some of the control variables might seem a bit far-fetched. This is a further sign that introspection is poor at working out what influences our thoughts and behaviour. We will see that holding a warm cup of coffee changes the way people perceive other people. Language impacts the McGurk effect – and perhaps some of the metaphors that we rely on. Crossing a scary bridge makes people more likely to fall in love. If we infer our own minds from the outside, as we will argue, our clothing could change our personality.

   You might be tempted to offer yourself as a sacrificial experimental subject. Unfortunately, if you finish this book you may be a poor subject. If you are leaving a psychology experiment and somebody accidentally knocks over a jar of pencils, you might guess that somebody else will count how many you pick up. There is a bit of an issue that many experiments are performed on undergraduate psychology students who are encouraged (compelled) to volunteer for experiments in return for course credit. Either the subjects are aware of the types of tricks that social psychologists use or they're not particularly interested in the field and one wonders why they're spending years of their life sitting exams in it.

2. (33). See also (102).
3. (79)
4. (157)
5. (11)
6. George Lakoff and Mark Johnson wrote an interesting book on this: (103)

7. (176)
8. (170)
9. (2)
10. The red/romance link affects both men's attraction to women (56) and women's attraction to men (55)
11. (30), (86)
12. (153), (20), (154)
13. The results couldn't be explained by the lonely students just being upset by the feedback or even grumpy with the experimenters for being unpleasant to them, because the researchers included a third condition in which the results apparently showed that the students were clumsy and likely to suffer severe accidents later in life. These students were just as upset by their news, but they were still generous and helpful.

    Believing that you are rejected, or will be in the future, seems to be self-fulfilling, leading to less pleasant behaviour to others, which presumably in turn leads to more rejection and ultimately a forlorn death bed. The one advantage that I can see to this unpleasant cycle is that it leaves you with more time to yourself, to read and ponder over paradoxes such as this one. Unfortunately, your pondering may also be of a lower quality.

    Students took the personality test and the experimenters gave them false feedback about their futures. The students then took mental reasoning tests. Those who'd been told that they were going to have a lonely old age did much worse on these and a series of difficult exams than those who'd been told that they would have a happy marriage.
14. (99)
15. (7). See also (152).
16. (108)
17. (113)
18. (109), (164), (27)
19. See (41) for discussion and experiments implanting (further) false memories in people who believe they've been abducted by aliens.

20. (174)

21. See (85) for an early review. The octagon experiment was published after this review and is in (101).

22. (39), (134). In another experiment (38), they showed a similar result. People are more likely to litter when the area is already littered (they gave unwitting participants the chance to litter by putting a handbill on their car windshields). This effect is even stronger when they see somebody else littering.

   In yet another experiment (74), Professor Cialdini and others designed towel-rack signs to encourage guests at a hotel to re-use their towels. One of their signs just asked customers to help the environment by reusing their towels. The other asked customers to join their fellow guests in helping to save the environment, telling them that 75% of other customers re-used their towels. Again, the most impactful sign was the one that mentioned what other people did. This time the message was helpful, increasing re-use rates by a quarter.

   In spite of all this evidence that telling people that others are doing something increases the likelihood they will do it themselves, it is still common for well-meaning groups, frustrated at the size of a problem, to tell everyone about it. (39) lists many examples including eating disorder programs, suicide prevention campaigns and high-school binge-drinking education efforts. They all had an adverse effect. While I was at university, the pro-life group distributed fliers telling students that one in three pregnancies ended in abortion. A shocking statistic, but I wonder whether the information increased or decreased the number of abortions. The research suggests that the message: 'Most women keep their babies: we can help you as we've helped others' would have been more effective.

23. (83)

24. (98)

25. (146)

26. Most large charities are aware of these effects, and target their

campaigns at our emotions rather than bombarding our reason with statistics. Some offer us the chance to sponsor or 'adopt' a poor child and show us photos of her, tell us the sports she likes to play, and print copies of drawings she's made, before telling us how hungry the little girl is, and how much she wants to go to school.

Even animal charities use similar techniques. In 2009, the RSPCA received over $100m in voluntary income, and spent over $20m on marketing. One of their mail shots has a kitten's face on the envelope and the question 'can YOU hear my cry for help?' In the enclosed letter, we learn that Stevie was just eight weeks old when his heartless owner threw him out. 'Cold and trembling, with a broken leg, his tiny mewing cries could barely be heard.'

If our charitable choices were reasoned, we'd want more information on the cost per rabbit re-homed so that we could compare it to the number of meals we could send to Ethiopians for the same amount. Some organisations do use such figures in their adverts, and it seems laudable, but any charity swapping their emotional appeal for statistical details doesn't understand human nature very well. And I'd prefer to donate to charities that understand humans.

27. (144)
28. See (76, 75, 82) for this section and the next.
29. (76, 75)
30. (97)
31. (111)
32. (96). See also (4).
33. (133)
34. There are many fascinating experiments on just-world theory. Two of the earliest are (105, 104). (80) is a recent review, including references to the final examples in the section.
35. In *Candide*, Voltaire wrote about an optimist, Pangloss, who contracted syphilis, lost an eye and an ear, and survived an earthquake and a tsunami before being hanged by the

Portuguese Inquisition for his heretical beliefs. Throughout the satire, Pangloss held to his philosophy that all was for the best in a world that must have been created for the best possible ends.

Pangloss's beliefs (actually a parody of those defended by Leibniz) were an attempt to deal with a sticky religious problem: if the world is created by a good god, how can there be evil in it?

36. (117)
37. (176)
38. (32, 139)
39. Some interesting discussion on the related ideas of neural re-use are in (6).
40. In fact, Leon Festinger and colleagues did the next best thing and infiltrated a millennial cult (64). This was perhaps less controversial than creating his own, as at worst they could be accused of failing to prevent harm to members rather than causing it.

On a similar note, one of my favourite books is by somebody who joined Scientology at an early stage in its development (95). It reads like a gripping thriller, but interested psychologists can play spot-the-technique as they read it.

41. e.g. (23, 24)
42. (84). Psychopaths are classified using a multi-item test. A cut-off is defined such that people with a higher score in the test are classed as psychopaths and those with a lower score are not. It is possible therefore to have many of the tendencies of a psychopath without being caught in the statistics, or indeed to define a cut-off that would classify a greater or smaller proportion of the population as psychopaths.

43. (162)
44. (155)
45. (88)
46. Researchers invent their own languages and teach them to volunteers (137, 138). Here is a list from one experiment. If you want

to play along, spend seven minutes memorising the following strings and then cover them up

| | | |
|---|---|---|
| XMXRTVTM | XXRVTM | XXRTVTM |
| VVTRTTVTM | XMMMMXM | VTVTRVTM |
| VTTTTVM | XMXRTTTVM | XMMMXRTVM |
| XXRTTTVM | XMMXRTVM | VVTRVM XMMXM |
| VTTTVTRVM | XMMMXRVTM | |

The list might have looked nonsensical, but there were actually rules governing which strings were possible. They had a grammar. The rules are complicated, and it would take me seven minutes to explain them to you. It would take even longer for you to memorise them.

I've not given you those rules, and working back to them from the list you've seen isn't trivial. But it might be that your unconscious brain has extracted some information. On the following page, there's another list of words. Half of the words are grammatically correct, the other half aren't. Put a tick next to the ones you think are right and a cross next to the others.

Artificial grammar strings

1. XMXRVM
2. VTTTVM
3. XMVRXRM
4. VVTRXRRRM
5. XMTRRM
6. VVRXRRM
7. XMMMXRVM
8. XXRTTVM
9. VTRRM
10. XMVTTRXM
11. VTTVTM
12. XMVRMVRXM
13. VVTRVTM
14. XMMXRVM
15. MXRTTVTM
16. VVTRTTVTM
17. XMVTRXRM
18. VTVTRTVM
19. XMMMXM
20. VTTTVTRVM
21. VVTTRMTM
22. XMVRXM
23. VVRMVTRXM
24. XXRTTVM
25. VVRMVRXM
26. XMVRXRRM
27. VTVTM
28. XMMXRTTVM
29. XMVRXRRRM
30. XMTRRRM

How confident are you that you did better than chance at this? Do you know what any of the rules are? Most people who take this test can't articulate any of them. They're confident on just a few of the strings. But on average, they get about two-thirds right. The answers, along with a discussion of the artificial grammar used, are below.

Our unconscious learns very fast. No French teacher could impart much grammar to me in seven minutes (they didn't manage much in five years), but without even knowing what we are supposed to be learning, we can grasp the rudiments of a difficult alien language.

Yet because we can't say what we've learned we don't have a lot of confidence. When researchers allow volunteers to gamble on which strings they know have the right grammar, betting either a high sum or a low sum, they don't do any better than chance at picking their winners. This seems to be a general characteristic of unconscious knowledge. When my dad took the stabilisers off my bike I was very unhappy. I had no idea how to stay upright. But he could see that I did.

The artificial grammar is defined by the following flow diagram.

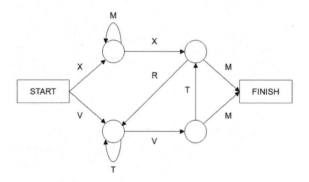

To use the diagram to create a string, start at the left-hand side. Now follow the arrows in the direction that they point.

Whenever you pass along an arrow, write down the letter next to the arrow. For example, begin by following the arrow marked X. Now go along the arrow at the top marked M. This arrow takes you back to where you started, so we can go along it again. M. Now let's follow the second X arrow. From here, take the R arrow, then the V arrow and finally the M arrow until we reach the end. Our string is XMMXRVM. If we can create a string with this diagram it's grammatically correct, if not then it isn't.

The correct strings are: 1, 2, 7, 8, 11, 13, 14, 15, 16, 18, 19, 20, 24, 27 and 28. Incidentally, the fifteen grammatically incorrect strings were all created using another grammar diagram. You might try working back from those strings to the diagram that created them. I predict you won't get very far in seven minutes.

### Comparison with English grammar

This artificial grammar might seem very artificial, but in structure it's a simplified version of real languages. The letters are equivalent to words and the strings are sentences. We could compose a simple flow diagram for constructing English.

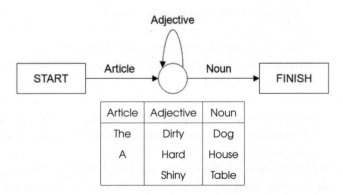

Using this, you can make sentences such as 'The Table', 'A Dirty House', and 'The Hard, Shiny Dog'. Some of them make more sense than others, but they're grammatically fine. But if you disobey the rules, you get something unacceptable. 'Hard A House' and 'Shiny Dog The' don't work.

English grammar is of course more complicated. Our diagram ignores subtleties even with the components that it includes. Take a simple sentence of the form article-adjective-adjective-noun. 'The big blue house' is okay. But there's something awkward about the sentence 'The blue big house'. You've probably never been taught that an adjective denoting size should come before one giving colour, but you use the rule anyway. Your unconscious brain knows it.

47. (106)

48. But whether verbalisation helps or hinders depends on the type of problem. Problems 1–2 required insight. The following problems are logical problems which you can crunch through.

   3. The police were convinced that either A, B, C or D had committed a crime.

      Each of the suspects, in turn, made a statement, but only one of the four statements was true. A said, 'I didn't do it.' B said, 'A is lying.' C said, 'B is lying.' D said, 'B did it.' Who is telling the truth, and who committed the crime?

   4. Three cards from an ordinary deck are lying on a table, face down. The following information (for some peculiar reason) is known about those three cards (all the following information refers to the same three cards). (i) To the left of the queen there is a jack. (ii) To the right of a spade there is a diamond. (iii) To the right of a heart there is a king. (iv) To the right of a king there is a spade. Can you assign the proper suit to each picture card?

Volunteers who tried these and similar problems didn't do any worse when thinking aloud, though they didn't do any better either. But something interesting happened when the experimenters gave the volunteers a hint. They told participants that sometimes people got stuck in a particular mindset, and that if they were having trouble it might be worth trying another approach.

On problems requiring insight (e.g. 1–2), or when volunteers worked quietly, the hint had no discernible effect. But when subjects worked on the problems that (i) could be crunched through and (ii) voiced their thought process, the hint dramatically harmed their success rate. The conscious mind confused itself and gave up too quickly on effective strategies. Thinking too hard and allowing your conscious mind to try too many lines of attack can be a bad thing.

Scientists found a similar result in a very different type of problem. Moderately able golfers practised putting up a gradual incline until they could get three balls in the hole in a row. Half of them then spent five minutes writing a detailed description of how they performed the task. The other half spoke about something unrelated.

Afterwards, they tried again to putt three balls in a row. Those who'd spoken about something unrelated achieved this in an average of eleven shots. The golfers who'd tried to explain what they were doing took twenty-one shots, which was just as many as when they first tried. Conscious reflection completely ruined all the benefits of practice.

It seems that there is an overhead to the unconscious problem-solver communicating with the conscious mind. In some problems this overhead slows the process down dramatically.

49. (50). This is a controversial experiment. Later in the book we'll see some similar experiments which scientists have used to claim that we need conscious attention to solve e.g. logical problems. However, the experiments of Dijksterhuis and colleagues are compelling. If we distract conscious attention and we are able to weigh information then we must be able to do this without conscious input. The converse isn't necessarily true. As all conscious processes are accompanied by unconscious processes (49), the distraction of conscious processes may also be distracting

unconscious processes, and it may be those which are needed to solve the test problem.

It may ultimately turn out that we need consciousness for some sorts of problems (indeed in this book I'll argue that this is so). However, the fact that we can solve some problems without conscious effort that we wrongly imagine we solve better with conscious effort is a dramatic result.

50. See e.g. (129) for a discussion of popular perceptions of subliminal advertising and the difficulties of using subliminal techniques in advertising. However, it is worth noting that advertising techniques where it is possible for targets to see the message, but where most of them don't and are still influenced, are widely used. The product placement experiments described in this book are one example. Banner adverts often go unnoticed, but still affect our choices when we don't recall seeing them (59).

51. (1)

52. (131)

53. (61)

54. Similar results came from Duke University, where Dasani was already market leader. With no exposures, 31% wanted Dasani as a gift. With twelve unnoticed exposures, 62% thought that nothing but Dasani could quench their thirst.

The unconscious can also do more than count the number of exposures we've had to a brand: it can also assess the relevance of these exposures. When the people in the pictures were out-group members (i.e. wearing kit from a different university) no increase in preference for Dasani was found.

Other experiments (59) have shown that banner adverts on Internet pages often go unnoticed, but still influence our preferences. The effect seems to rely on an increased fluency leading to a positive experience, which we misattribute as a preference for the brand. So noticing the adverts / product placement and understanding why we have the fluency may actually damage their effectiveness. This presents a problem for sophisticated advertisers explaining their strategy to management. Who wants to hear they've spent millions on a campaign and nobody even noticed the ads? Perhaps the disbelieving managers might offer to subliminally prime the ad-men with images of money instead of paying them so that they have the impression of being rich.

55. The following exercise is based on one given by John Bargh and colleagues(12).

From each set of five words below, make a grammatically-correct four-word sentence.

For example, from the list:

*good cat she very was*

you could form the sentence:

*she was very good*

If you are able to, time yourself on the task and see how quickly you can complete the exercise.

1. father sat TV likes my
2. apple the please rules respect
3. the was optimistic flat patient
4. flock sensitively granddad her told
5. tomorrow usually her they see
6. I ready discreetly was not
7. exercised bald dog Sally her
8. cautiously will golf play I
9. grass green the off keep
10. weight hair brown I have
11. here yield in it lives
12. optimistically this have finished I

Given the topic of this book, you might have guessed that there's something more to this exercise than a test of your language abilities. If you look back at the lists, you will see that half of them contain words loosely associated with politeness: *respect, sensitively, discreetly, cautiously, yield, optimistically*. As you worked quickly to complete the unscrambling, you probably didn't notice the connection between these words. But your brain will have. When John Bargh and colleagues gave a similar exercise to volunteers (who weren't expecting to be primed), their behaviour changed, as described in the main body of the book.

56. (12)

57. It might equally be that I infer that I want to finish this book by observing the fact that I'm sitting here tapping away. The unconscious might in fact be following a goal of postponing a difficult conversation with my wife, in which case my inference about my book-finishing goal would be wrong. This is the subject matter of Part Three.

58. (34). A short review of unconscious goal pursuit is (45).

59. (115). In fact the effect has been found to be weaker for Japanese listeners (140). It may be that Japanese listeners depend less on visual cues when listening.

60. e.g. *http://www.youtube.com/watch?v = P vHRkB37aE*

61. (141, 142)

62. (3). (81) deals with some confounds: in the original experiment, the smaller discs were closer to the poker chip than the larger discs, which distorted the effect.

63. (26)

64. These results are consistent with those from earlier, more gruesome experiments. Through the Sixties, Dr Delgado operated on the brains of animals and humans (47). To do this, the doctor removed part of their skulls under local anaesthetic (think of the scene in the film *Hannibal* for an idea of what this looks like in a non-clinical setting). Dr Delgado didn't offer his patients a taste of their prefrontal cortex, but while their brains were open he did insert electrodes.

By passing current through these electrodes, he could alter aspects of their behaviour. In one case, he was able to make the patient move. This wasn't a sudden, jerky movement, but apparently normal, smooth head and body turning. In spite of the doctor's control, his patient remained convinced that the movements were spontaneous. When Dr Delgado asked them what they were doing, the patient replied: 'I am looking for my slippers,' 'I heard a noise,' and 'I am restless.'

65. You might have noticed that the decisions made in the finger-extending experiment were very fast. You might argue that perhaps in slower decisions we do make a conscious decision first. We shall see later in the book that we often do have conscious knowledge of our actions before we begin them – and need to do so if consciousness is to be of any use. We still don't make conscious decisions, but we do use consciousness to check that a decision is socially acceptable.

66. (166)

67. (149)

68. (125)

69. (112)

70. (63, 62)

71. A similar experiment found that children also know how important reward is in motivating behaviour (100). Teams of children played games. When they won prizes for doing well, they said that they enjoyed the games less (than players in a separate competition for which prizes weren't given) even though they hadn't expected the prizes when they played. I wonder whether this is why I found pass-the-parcel so dull as a child.

72. (22)

73. (54)

74. It's possible to imagine alternative explanations for these results. Perhaps the frightening bridge was in a more romantic site and it was these feelings which were transferred to the experimenter, or maybe the high bridge attracted thrill-seeking tourists who were by their nature more likely to try their luck with her. The researchers therefore tried to get the same results in the laboratory.

Participants, all male heterosexuals, believed that they were taking part in a series of experiments to test the effects of electric shocks on learning. They would do this at the same time as another subject. In fact, the other subject was always an attractive female chosen by the experimenters. There were two different levels of shock that could be applied: a weak, tingling one and a strong, painful one. The participants tossed a coin to decide which level of shock they would experience, and were then sent away while the experimenter set up the equipment.

While the participants waited for the shock experiment, they completed a questionnaire and wrote a creative story. Those who were expecting strong shocks wrote stories with more sexual content, said that they were more likely to ask out the pretty girl also doing the experiment, and admitted to a stronger desire to kiss her.

Interestingly, the experimenters also included a condition in which instead of using a pretty girl as the second subject they used a man. Subjects who were paired with a man expressed much more anxiety about the upcoming shocks than those paired with the girl. They answered questions about this in a private cubicle, so the less fearful men weren't just acting macho in front of the woman they'd decided they wanted to kiss. It seems that the threat of shocks caused sweaty hands and a throbbing heart in all the men. Those who were in the presence of an attractive woman thought they were due to sexual attraction, but those who weren't had to attribute them to fear.

75. (94)
76. The film *Twelve Angry Men* is a riveting exploration of how hard it is to support a view when everybody else is against it. One of the most famous experiments showing conformity was Solomon Asch's (8) experiment on the judgement of the length of lines. He presented three lines of different lengths and a fourth line, which matched that of one of the others. One of the participants was the subject, and the others were all stooges. The stooges gave an incorrect answer to the question of which of the three lines the fourth matched. Most of the subjects gave an incorrect answer to at least one question (but by no means all). This question had a clear objective answer (error rates without social

pressure were tiny): the fact that people conformed at all is amazing. Some of the subjects knew they were conforming with the others, others thought retrospectively that they had answered correctly. Even when they answered correctly they were often visibly uncomfortable.

I had a teacher who repeated this experiment for us. He sent a boy out of the classroom for talking. While the boy was out, he briefed us and called the lad back into the classroom. Later in the lesson, the teacher drew up three lines as part of a set of 'illusions' and asked us each what we saw. After several people had said that the shorter line was longest he asked the boy who had earlier been sent out. He did indeed claim that he also thought the shorter line was longest – and sparked a fascination with psychology in at least one of his classmates.

Interestingly, the teacher claimed his demonstration never failed. In Asch's experiment, many of the subjects did give correct answers. It would be fascinating to know whether the added pressure of real peers increased the effect, whether my teacher was good at choosing people who would conform, or whether being sent out of class beforehand increased the pressure on the subject to fit in afterwards.

Given that we frequently conform on objective questions, it is not surprising that we so often conform on questions where the answer is less clear cut: which is most of the things we think of as forming culture.

77. The foot-in-the-door technique (67), much studied in the field of social compliance (40), is the standard demonstration of this. In the first step, subjects are asked to comply with some small request, such as putting a badge for a charity on their bag (35). In the second step, participants are asked for a larger action, such as helping out on a stall for three hours. With the larger request, participants are typically unwilling to help just because they have been asked. However, acceding to the initial smaller request generally leads to higher participation rates (29).

78. (43, 73)

79. Pardon the pun.
80. (166)
81. (13)
82. (14)
83. Recent research suggests that infants may have an understanding of other people's minds earlier than this, which they are, for some reason, unable to verbalise. A discussion of this is in (148).
84. (130)
85. You might argue that the autistic children do not fail the Smarties test because they have a deficit in their understanding of their own mental states, but rather because they fail to appreciate that the experimenter will be able to catch them out lying about their earlier knowledge. However, other experiments such as (132) show that this is not the root of their problem. A fascinating article by Frith and Happé discusses in more depth the problems autistic children have in understanding their own minds (68). See also (171).
86. (10)
87. Incidentally, as the addicts were prepared to pay more when they were craving than when they had taken the drug, it confirms that avoidance of withdrawal is a bigger driver of their addiction than the pleasant experience that got them hooked in the first place. Beware kids!
88. (136, 135, 37)
89. (158, 159)
90. (175)
91. This question was put by Ap Dijksterhuis (49).
92. There is much literature on the subject. A good review is (57).
93. This experiment (15) is one of the trippiest I have ever read about. The participants were describing the ball-bearings to a teddy bear wearing a blindfold. Because some people clam up when asked to talk to a stuffed toy they had practice sessions first in which they told him about a tower they were building and described cartoon villains such as Cruella de Vil and Captain Hook. Unfortunately, the experimenters felt it appropriate to exclude data from one participant who 'seemed to be unusually flippant

about the task, calling the bear "Mister Bear" and at one point even naming a marble "Bob".' But with or without this participant's contribution, there was a big difference in the way that volunteers who had control over the magnets and those who didn't described what was happening.

94. Whether or not such minds really exist.
95. (46)
96. See (107) for a controversial experiment showing that conscious reactions are slow.
97. The standard test is the implicit association test (IAT) (77, 126). But others include making quick decisions about whether somebody is holding a gun (44, 128), in which white people typically choose in a way that indicates a less favourable attitude towards black people, and one that suggests the use of a stereotype that black people are aggressive.

    An interesting study shows that subliminally priming white subjects with images of black faces causes them to be more aggressive in interactions over a phone (36). In this experiment, subjects have no way of knowing that the stereotype is causing their behaviour.

98. For example, Fazio et al. (60) found that measures of explicit racism (a questionnaire) correlated with subjects' opinions on the Rodney King verdict and the justifiability of the ensuing anger in the black community. However, their implicit measure of racism was a better predictor of subjects' friendliness towards a black experimenter. In the absence of a control test, it would have been impossible for the subjects to infer that their friendliness or otherwise towards the black experimenter was caused by the race of the experimenter.

    Our conscious attitudes can only be applied when (i) there is time for our self-model to be consulted, and (ii) it is possible for our social model of ourselves to infer from our choice of behaviour that they have or haven't been applied.

99. (156)
100. (171)

101. An interesting aspect of the work was that nearly all of those who chose a poster without giving reasons chose a picture by Monet or Van Gogh. About a third of those who gave reasons chose a humorous poster. It is noticeable that people who talk a lot about art and literature like different art and books to the rest of us. A cynic might argue that conceptual art is easy to talk about rather than intrinsically attractive and that this is the source of its apparent popularity among those who like to discuss art.

102. We only infer other people's minds so that we can work out what they will do before they do it. But we can only use information from what they have already done (and the situation etc.).

103. See for example the discussion on the 'language of the eyes' in (13).

104. (87)

105. (28)

106. Or a switch in my visual attention. If I spill water, it is plausible that my brain could send a signal that what has happened is socially relevant and ensure that visual cues (which an outside observer will share) are sent to consciousness. Later in this part, we will examine evidence that the brain is able to select socially relevant information and make it accessible to the model that produces consciousness.

107. (66, 92)

108. (145)

109. Analogous results are also found among experienced typists. Experimenters inserted errors into subjects' typing, and corrected some actual errors (110). The typists slowed marginally when they had actually erred. However, they were as likely to believe that the artificially corrected words had been typed correctly as words that they had indeed typed correctly.

110. There are lots of scenarios where having access to private knowledge that cannot be inferred by counterparts improves our ability to predict and manipulate the behaviour of other people. There is information that other people will later find out (e.g. I burnt a hole in my wife's dress while ironing it). There is information

that other people might already know (e.g. my wife might have seen the dress when getting changed). There is also information that I can choose to communicate (e.g. that I burnt a hole in the dress and that I have booked a table for dinner on Saturday after she's had time to buy a new one).

A further reason to selectively incorporate knowledge that others don't have access to is the problem of multiple interaction partners. In the changing-room example above, my friend has the knowledge that my stuff is in locker 87. The man at locker 87 will probably infer the knowledge when we march towards him. But the other occupants of the changing room will not have this information until later, and some of the men we pass will never know it. We could hypothetically build a separate model of ourselves for each person we interact with, but it seems simpler to build one shared model and incorporate adjustments to this model in terms of explicit knowledge that other people are mistaken about. One of these adjustments, that of false beliefs, seems to be what is tested in the Smarties and Sally / Anne experiments (14, 130).

A social model of ourselves that *only* incorporated knowledge that other people are likely to have about us might seem to be a purer model. But a self-model that has access to some information that is not available to other people is more effective at giving us advice on what other people will infer about us and how we can manipulate and respond to their behaviour.

111. (165)

112. You could improve the robot a bit. When there's more light at the front than the back it would be nice if the back wheels weren't trying to pull it backwards. You could add a circuit that turned them off when this happens. Now you seem to have a central decision maker. It compares the amount of light seen in front of it to that behind it and decides which set of wheels should be running.

But in practice this decision maker is some kind of switch. There are electrical signals coming from the front of the machine and more coming from the back. Depending on the comparative strength of these signals it sends an electrical current of its own. The decision maker doesn't need to know what is causing these signals or what the effect of its own signal is. It could be a switch in a mobile phone, a computer or a toaster.

So knowing the state of this switch doesn't negate the need for a model. The model still needs to understand how the electrical signals received by this switch relate to the inputs and how the signals sent correspond to the outputs. If it knows all this, it doesn't need to know what the switch is actually doing at all: it just needs to know which wheels are moving and how fast. It can infer the state of the switch from this information, and access to the actual state of the switch doesn't add anything.

113. Morsella and colleagues (120, 122, 121) have noted this difference between what we are and are not conscious of. Morsella (120) lists examples of conflicts between competing systems that are resolved unconsciously, including the McGurk effect (115), binocular rivalry, and depth perception.

114. e.g. (51)

115. e.g. (65)

116. There are many further examples of actions we usually make automatically becoming conscious when there is a conflict making it socially interesting. We generally reach for a glass of water without noticing that we are doing so, but if we have an injury we become aware of our actions. Again, there are social questions which could affect the effort I should put into reaching for the glass. Will you help me if my injured arm prevents me from reaching the cup? Will you infer that I'm exaggerating my injury because I'm lazy? Should I risk damaging myself further to hide my injury because you will take advantage of my weakness if you notice it?

117. Because scientists don't get enough invites to parties, they have confirmed the results in the lab. In 1959, Moray described the 'cocktail party effect' (119). Moray played subjects two messages of equal intensity, one through each ear, asking subjects to repeat

out loud the list played in one ear. Generally, participants blocked out the message in the other ear, and could recall no content from that message. However, when the recording in the ignored ear included a message preceded by the subjects' name, the subjects were frequently aware of that message.

This experiment is consistent with other studies showing that conscious perception of stimuli is affected by the social significance of the stimuli, such as in perceptual defence (114, 58).

118. See (52, 53) for discussion of the social brain hypothesis.

119. (78)

120. I've been lucky to have some very good bosses. One of the best explained to me that he no longer produced anything directly himself. His job was therefore about working out how to get other people, some of whom he thought were smarter than himself, to do the work for him. He spent all day thinking about what motivated one person or why another turned up in the mornings. He thought about what he could do to explain something to somebody else and why another pair didn't seem to get on. He described management as a profoundly humble experience, where the only ego that didn't matter was his own. (Given his benignly Machiavellian view, I wondered what he was hoping to change about me by telling me this.) The least effective boss I've known took the opposite perspective: that he'd made it and the role of his employees was to guess what he wanted. I can see the advantage to the employees of taking this view, but not of the firm hiring such a manager who, while technically very talented, never understood why he had such high employee turnover.

121. Peter Carruthers' (31) arguments are most close to this, 'metacognition, on this view, results from turning one's mindreading capacities upon oneself, its emergence will be a byproduct of the evolution of mindreading'. (Metacognition being 'cognition about one's own cognition' – he also distinguishes between access consciousness and phenomenal consciousness.) He allows that metacognition might have come under 'secondary' selection later.

However, without considering the selection, I think the important asymmetries between the way we infer our own mind and those of others cannot be adequately accounted for. Nor that information in a form that can be used by the mind inference machinery (with necessary omissions) is prepared and made available to it.

122. Baumeister and Masicampo discuss a possible social purpose of consciousness (17) (see also (18)) differing somewhat from that proposed in this book. They argue that consciousness 'enables communication across different parts of the mind and brain' – a common part of several theories that I discuss in the following endnotes. However, they also note the close connection between conscious thought and speech, and recognise that social needs probably drove the evolution of conscious thought.

Nicholas Humphrey also developed a theory (89) which connected consciousness to a social purpose. In this, our own experience allows us to understand our own behaviour. Because it allows us to understand ourselves, we are better able to understand other people: 'the explanation we have of our own behaviour could then form the basis for explaining other people's, too'. (So by feeling pain and knowing how we respond to it, we can understand what other people will do in such a situation.) Humphrey himself seems to have moved on from this idea, which he developed long before most of the experiments in this book were conducted (see (90)).

123. In this work, we have not considered all the many theories of consciousness that exist. There are books (e.g. (160)) that compile various theories of what consciousness does for us, some of them decidedly odd.

124. Bernard Baars (9) argues that 'consciousness might help to mobilize and integrate brain functions that are otherwise separate and independent'. The conscious access theory has gained some support.

Certain evidence claimed in support of this theory is also consistent with the current theory. Consciousness does integrate information from many processes, as I argue in the main text.

That it needs to do so in order to serve its role doesn't show that this is its role.

Other evidence compares results from similar tasks done without awareness and with awareness. In some cases, the differences might be due to the strength of the input. When the input is small (e.g. a word presented for a few milliseconds) the brain responds in one, simple way. When the input is larger (e.g. a word presented for longer), the brain reacts in a more effortful way, processing it in other parts of the brain unrelated to consciousness but also sending a signal to the self-model to work out what the social implications of the word are. It could be that consciousness and certain other brain processes are costly and the brain only makes use of them when it is worthwhile. That consciousness is set in motion on a problem at the same time as other processes doesn't show that consciousness is needed to set the other processes in motion or to integrate the results of these processes.

Dissociation experiments are also used in support of other possible roles for consciousness. I think the results of these are suggestive rather than conclusive. In this experimental paradigm (e.g. (48)), subjects' consciousness is given either a heavy distracting load by e.g. counting backwards from 917 in sixes (19), or a lesser load such as counting forward in single digits. If the subject is more or less able to perform some task under the heavy load, then a role for consciousness (positive or negative) is inferred. However, consciousness definitely relies on many other processes feeding into it. It may be that one of these other processes is also being distracted in the heavy load condition and that it is this which interferes with the tested task. The paradigm of the dissociation tasks places great weight on the assumption that all unconscious systems are parallel with infinite capacity and also homogenous (unconscious loads which may have been more or less relevant to the task did not affect the task (48)).

An experiment that suggests that the assumptions made in the dissociation paradigm may not be appropriate used distractors to moderate the McGurk effect. The McGurk effect (115) is a preconscious effect in which visual cues and auditory cues are combined to form a conscious percept. Alsius et al. (5) asked participants to attend to a series of beeps while watching a video of a woman mouthing one syllable when another syllable had been dubbed over the audio recording. If the dissociation paradigm is correct, we might expect that the conscious load of counting beeps would not interfere with the unconscious processes underlying the effect. Alternatively, we might expect the beeps to degrade the auditory signal and increase the visual effect (a control experiment showed that playing white noise over the auditory recording did just this). But in fact the conscious auditory distractor reduced the McGurk effect and led to dramatically more conscious reports of the auditory syllable.

We also believe that some processes may be consciously accessible not because consciousness is needed to perform them but because we need to be able to communicate reliably about these processes. So with the type of instinctive reasoning in Maier's experiment (112), the answer is all that really matters. Our inferred (incorrect) reasoning process should correspond with other people's, but does not have to be accurate. In logical problem-solving, we may need to be able to communicate the steps in order to convince other people of the correctness of our conclusions. Things that may need to be communicated must necessarily interact with our social model.

Nevertheless, we would be surprised if conscious thought did not do more than provide us with a socially useful model of ourselves, however impressive and useful that role is. The tools that go into creating a social model of ourselves are tremendously powerful, and presumably costly. It might be that the same processes that infer our mind, combining many sources of information, are useful for logical reasoning, say, and have been adapted to do so. Our conscious awareness of the steps would then be an artefact of the origin of the process that we use for logical reasoning.

125. Supramodular interaction theory (SIT) (120, 122, 121) is a particular theory which claims that consciousness is needed to integrate certain types of information and form a final decision. By considering this particular theory, which carefully considers and avoids some of the more obvious weaknesses in a general conscious access theory, in some more depth, we'll highlight our general objections to this class of theory.

The theory posits that there are a number of response systems, each consisting of a number of modules, and each with a single concern. These supramodular systems concerns have direct skeletal muscle tendencies. For example, a tissue-damage system can directly, and without conscious mediation, cause us to pull our hand away from a hot object. However, different systems can have conflicting demands on skeletomotor action. The authors of SIT argue that phenomenal states are needed for producing integrated action, which they define as follows (121): 'Integrated action occurs when two (or more) action plans that could normally influence behaviour on their own (when existing at the level of activation) are simultaneously co-activated and trying to influence the same skeletal muscle effector.'

I will outline four reasons for preferring the present theory over supramodular interaction theory. The fourth is a direct difference in apparent empirical predictions between the two theories, which I believe has been tested experimentally.

Firstly, if phenomenal states are needed for integrated action then it is a feature that we likely share with much of the animal kingdom. Salamanders, for example, have to weigh their desire for food against their risk of being eaten while they search for it. Whitham and Mathis (169) show that hungrier salamanders forage more frequently, but do so less when the experimenters add hormones of a natural predator to the water. The conflict salamanders face and resolve is of the type described in supramodular integration theory. Similarly, every time a predator decides whether to conserve energy or to continue hunting, or a male decides whether to fight for a mate or to avoid tissue damage, they are settling conflicts of the type described in SIT. It is possible that salamanders use a different mechanism to deal with conflicting action plans. However, it is not clear why humans should have replaced an old and effective system, which successfully navigates the same types of conflict in other animals. The suggestion implicit in SIT that salamanders and other simple animals are phenomenally aware is not in itself a reason to reject the theory, but it is an implication which is easily overlooked.

Secondly, SIT does not explain (and does not attempt to explain, being a correlational analysis) why we should be phenomenally aware of the process that integrates the output of the supramodules. Within the proposed supramodules there are many conflicts which are resolved unconsciously. Morsella (120) lists examples of these including the McGurk effect (115), binocular rivalry and depth perception. These effects are not obviously less complex than the conflicts that SIT deals with. The consistent difference is that they cannot directly cause skeletal muscle action. Yet it is not clear within SIT why this particular sort of conflict, and no other type of conflict, gives rise to consciousness. Unlike the theory described in this paper, SIT is unable to explain the phenomenal aspect of phenomenal states. (Within the social theory of consciousness presented in this book, the connection between consciousness and skeletal muscle actions is clear: it is skeletal muscle actions which typically have social consequences.)

Thirdly, SIT does not explain why we are so often unaware of why we make decisions. If consciousness is an aware decision maker how can it not be aware of which decisions it makes and how it makes them? Why should it be tricked into thinking that it chose the left stocking because of the quality of the knit? Why does it invent reasons for why we picked one jam over another? These are not readily explainable by SIT and would be fundamental flaws in a system that is designed to choose one course of action over another by integrating conflicting information.

Finally, we examine a difference in the predictions that the explanation in this paper and SIT make. The theory presented in this book claims that the social model of ourselves, which produces consciousness, is one of several inputs that go into a decision. SIT, on the other hand, claims that 'one is aware of (. . .) the computational processes underlying the interaction of system outputs' (120). In SIT, phenomenal states are the final point at which the decision is made between possible competing actions, and we are aware of what goes into making this decision.

In our theory, it is possible that the advice formed in consciousness is overridden, and we will be unaware of the reason that it is overridden (though we will then infer why we made this decision, and we will be aware of the inferred, possibly incorrect, reasoning). In SIT, this is not possible. It should not be possible in SIT to 'prime one system to counter the tendencies of another system' (120).

A handgrip experiment (131) (also discussed in the body of the book) appears to provide an initial test of this scenario directly. In a series of trials, subjects squeezed a handgrip on cue. Each trial was worth a penny or a pound. A thermometer showed how much force participants were exerting, and the greater the force, the greater the proportion of the purse the participants were able to keep. After each trial, subjects saw their accumulated total.

This seems to be a conflict of the type that SIT envisages. The competing responses are to squeeze hard (to attain the maximum reward for the trial) and to avoid fatigue (directly relevant given the sequence of trials). When participants were supraliminally presented with the reward before each trial, they squeezed the handgrip harder on the pound trials, demonstrating the existence of the conflict.

However, participants also squeezed harder on trials with subliminal presentation of the monetary award. This result appears to be in conflict with the predictions of SIT.

One could, in principle, argue that the money primes influenced the supramodule that initiates action. The impulse to squeeze on penny trials was perhaps less powerful and therefore more easily overwhelmed by the impulse to avoid fatigue. However, if all the information necessary to manage the conflict is contained in the signals from the supramodules then it is not clear what role the supramodular integration system (phenomenal state) plays beyond the comparison of the strength of two signals.

I argue that it is easier to explain the correlational analysis of Morsella and Bargh in terms of our theory that consciousness arises from our social model. In our theory, conflicts play an especially interesting role. It is possible that the advice from our social model can conflict with other drivers of our action. For example, we may hold our hand in cold water to win a prize or please an experimenter, but we will ultimately pull our hand out of the water to avoid tissue damage. Similarly, our social model may advise us to stop smoking or avoid having another slice of cake, but other signals in the brain may lead us to fail. This type of conflict has been heavily studied (123), and we note that managing the conflicts is energy intensive (71), and that the outcome can be influenced by unconscious primes (150).

To create the social model, we must integrate a large quantity of information from our different senses and the output of other processing systems. But we argue that integration of this information is necessary to produce consciousness rather than vice-versa. The type of information that is integrated is a function of the social model's purpose rather than being of a special type that only consciousness can deal with.

126. My claim, as set out earlier, is that a narrower set of things enter consciousness. We don't have conscious access to all the information necessary to infer the states. Instead, it is generally the inferred states (e.g. that we like somebody) themselves that we are conscious of rather than what goes into creating these inferences (e.g. that they are mimicking us). Some of the things we have conscious access to -- such as vision – might seem to fall outside this. However, vision is a state we do attribute to others.

We might say John got up and left because he saw Julie enter. So to understand what others are inferring about us we do need to know what we see as a state of the model not just as an input to the inference.

127. There are a number of ways that we can try to understand behaviour and consciousness experimentally. Some of these offer fairly direct evidence, others are more suggestive than conclusive. To see why this is so, let's consider four classes of experiment.

   1. If we manipulate a group of subjects and their behaviour changes versus that of controls, we can be fairly sure that the manipulation caused the change in behaviour. For example, if we hit fifty subjects on the nose and they all step back, but we treat fifty other subjects identically but don't hit them on the nose and they don't step back we can be fairly sure that hitting people on the nose causes people to step back, at least in the situation we're studying (you might get a different answer in a boxing ring).

   2. If we manipulate a group of subjects and their conscious reports change versus controls then we can be fairly sure that the manipulation causes a change in their conscious reports. (Note that conscious reports are a form of behaviour; we have assumed throughout this book that conscious reports correspond to an underlying consciousness that it is sensible to talk about. Conscious reports are a measurable signal. The existence of consciousness is an inference. Science relies on measuring signals. When a physicist talks about an electron he's inferring its presence because it is the best way she has to explain the signals she measures.) So if the fifty subjects we bop on the nose report liking us less than the fifty we don't, we can be fairly sure that hitting someone on the nose leads them to report liking you less. If we're happy to assume that conscious reports reflect an underlying consciousness then we can also infer that hitting someone on the nose leads to a conscious dislike of the person hitting them on the nose (again with the same limitations to the situation).

3. If we manipulate a group of subjects and their conscious reports do NOT change, but their behaviour does, we can be fairly sure that the manipulation changes their behaviour through unconscious processes. Because our manipulation changes behaviour, we are in case (1). But because there is no change in conscious reports, and if we are happy with our assumption that conscious reports reflect an underlying consciousness, we can rule out any hypothesis that a change in the contents of consciousness led to the behaviour. Note that we can use this method to investigate changes in conscious reports too. For example, the mimicking experiments led to changes in conscious reports. If you mimic a group of people they will report liking you better than the group you don't mimic. However, because they report being unaware that you were mimicking them, we can rule out certain mechanisms which led to the change in liking.

4. If we manipulate a group of subjects and their conscious reports do change and so also does their behaviour, we CANNOT infer that the change in consciousness led to their change in behaviour. So if we hit our fifty subjects on the nose and they all step back and report liking us less we cannot be sure that hitting them on the nose led them to dislike us and this dislike led them to step back from us, however tempting it is. (Indeed the slowness of consciousness and the quickness of stepping back may allow us to rule it out in this case.) It is possible that the manipulation changes both behaviour and conscious report independently.

For example, some studies try and show a use for consciousness by presenting a stimulus subliminally to one group of participants and supraliminally to another group. The behaviour of the second group is different to that of the first group and so are the conscious reports (they are able to report seeing the stimuli). The claim is that this demonstrates a causal role for consciousness in changing behaviour. However, this claim is not justified. It may be that the extended presentation of the stimuli to the second group changes their behaviour (other than the conscious report) through unconscious mechanisms, and also, separately, leads to a change in the contents of consciousness.

Another attempt to separate the effect of conscious and unconscious processes leads to strongly suggestive, but not conclusive, evidence that we use consciousness for logical reasoning. In one experimental paradigm (48), subjects are given either a heavy distracting load by e.g. counting backwards from 917 in sixes (19), or a lesser load such as counting forward in single digits. If the subject is more or less able to perform some task under the heavy load, then a role for consciousness (positive or negative) is inferred. Logical reasoning is one of the things we are less able to do under a heavy load. However, consciousness relies on many other processes feeding into it. It may be that one of these other processes is also being distracted in the heavy load condition and that it is this which interferes with the tested task. The experimental paradigm places great weight on the assumption that all unconscious systems are parallel with infinite capacity and also homogenous (unconscious loads which may have been more or less relevant to the task did not affect the task (48)).

128. See (6) for examples and a discussion of neural re-use generally.
129. e.g. (33)
130. (151). It is notable that the areas in which people with high self-control excel are in social achievements. We also note that there are individual differences in the levels of people's self-control. Measurements made in childhood are predictive of self-control in adulthood (143).
131. (124)
132. (161)
133. For a review see (21). Other effects include: (i) making choices uses the same mental muscles as self-control. Volunteers who choose between alternative shampoos, T-shirts and socks are less able to hold their hands in cold water for long periods of time (161). (ii) Occasionally, an exercise that exhausts our mental muscles can improve our score on a subsequent test. Participants

who depleted themselves on one task claimed to have done better than others on a second task, which they marked themselves and for which they were paid (116). Avoiding the temptation to cheat also seems to require willpower.

134. (70)

135. (127)

136. Other self-control exercises, reviewed in (16), also develop our willpower. Improving your posture whenever you realise you're slouching or closely monitoring your finances will improve your self-control generally as well as giving you a straight back and a better bank balance.

But some exercises have very little impact. Improving your mood when you feel down takes self-control, but regularly doing so won't increase your willpower. In fact, the research group that discovered most of what we know about willpower estimate that only about half of their attempted interventions are successful.

This shouldn't surprise us. Not all physical exercise routines are equally effective either. A swimmer can improve his times with a well-designed gym routine; but a swimming regime won't greatly help you to lift weights. Holding a book above my head until my arms drop may test my stamina, but it's not necessarily the most efficient way to improve it.

137. (168)

138. (71)

139. (42). Another study (93) manipulated beliefs that willpower was a limited resource generally, and found similar results: those who believed that they would have sufficient resources used them. These studies show that our beliefs about our abilities influence our motivation to continue exerting willpower and the point at which we will give up and work out how to justify our failure. Some recent discussion of this is in (91). An alternative explanation, that these studies show that the belief that willpower is limited cause it to be limited, and there is no underlying resource being used up, is not consistent with experiments showing that sugary drinks (and not artificially sweetened placebos) restore it, e.g. (71,

72). However, on this we note that there is recent evidence that swilling a sugary juice around the mouth can improve self-control (and athletic effort) (118). This suggests that it may not be merely glucose levels in the blood that mediates self-control. It may be that the brain is prepared to use up more of its limited energy resources when it is assured that further supplies are on the way.

140. (150)

141. (25)

142. Other animals certainly modify their behaviour to change the behaviour of other animals. However, it is not yet clear whether any of them have the social models that we rely on, and therefore consciousness.

You might argue that you shave because you yourself prefer the way you look without so much hair. However, inasmuch as this is a conscious preference, it is really a preference aimed at changing the way other people perceive you.

143. There is a certain circularity in this argument. When I say achieve more, I am implicitly talking about doing the things that improve our lot in the eyes of the world, i.e. socially. If the model that produces consciousness is aimed at doing this, then following its advice more often should have the desired effect. The trade-off that might have existed more often in the past between building social capital and eating or taking fewer risks with our life are probably rarer today.

144. Many of the following examples in this section are described in greater detail in (69). The article describes many further links between glucose levels, and our metabolism of glucose, and self-control.

145. (161)

146. Reference in (69).

147. (147)

148. Reference in (69).

149. (173)

150. There are some truly great writers who realise that our

explanation of why we are doing what we are doing comes after we have done it.

*I cannot fix on the hour, or the spot, or the look, or the words, which laid the foundation. It is too long ago. I was in the middle before I knew that I had begun.*

> Mr Darcy, when Elizabeth asked him to explain why he had fallen in love with her.
> *Pride and Prejudice*, Jane Austen

In 'I love the way you lie', Eminem raps, 'I can't tell you what it really is, I can only tell you what it feels like,' which may be a deep reflection on the separation between the unconscious that controls us and what we are consciously aware of and able to report. In his song he later discusses the separation between his (conscious) intentions and expectations and what really happens.

# REFERENCES

(1) H. AARTS, R. CUSTERS, AND H. MARIEN. Preparing and motivating behavior outside of awareness. *Science*, **319**(5870): 1639–1639, 2008.

(2) J. M. ACKERMAN, C. C. NOCERA, AND J. A. BARGH. Incidental haptic sensations influence social judgments and decisions. *Science*, **328**:1712–1714, 2010.

(3) S. AGLIOTI, J. F. X. DESOUZA, AND M. A. GOODALE. Size-contrast illusions deceive the eye but not the hand. *Current Biology*, **5**(6):679–685, 1995.

(4) M. D. ALICKE. Culpable causation. *Journal of Personality and Social Psychology*, **63**(3):368–378, 1992.

(5) A. ALSIUS, J. NAVARRA, R. CAMPBELL, AND S. SOTO-FARACO. Audiovisual integration of speech falters under high attention demands. *Current Biology*, **15**(9):839–843, 2005.

(6) M. L. ANDERSON. Neural reuse: A fundamental organizational principle of the brain. *Behavioral and Brain Sciences*, **33**(4):245–313, 2010.

(7) J. ANTONAKIS AND O. DALGAS. Predicting elections: Child's play. *Science*, **323**:1183, 2009.

(8) S. E. ASCH. Opinions and social pressure. *Scientific American*, **193**(5):31–35, 1955.

(9) B. J. BAARS. The conscious access hypothesis: Origins and recent evidence. *Trends in Cognitive Sciences*, **6**(1):47–52, 2002.

(10) G. J. BADGER, W. K. BICKEL, L. A. GIORDANO, E. A. JACOBS, G. LOEWENSTEIN, AND L. MARSCH. Altered states: The impact of immediate craving on the valuation of current and future opioids. *Journal of Health Economics*, **26**(5):865–876, 2007.

(11) J. N. BAILENSON AND N. YEE. Digital chameleons. *Psychological Science*, 16:814–819, 2005.

(12) J. A. BARGH, M. CHEN, AND L. BURROWS. Automaticity of social behavior: Direct effects of trait construct and stereotype activation on action. *Journal of Personality and Social Psychology*, 71(2):230–244, 1996.

(13) S. BARON-COHEN. *Mindblindness: An essay on autism and theory of mind*. MIT Press, 1997.

(14) S. BARON-COHEN, A. M. LESLIE, AND U. FRITH. Does the autistic child have a 'theory of mind'? *Cognition*, 21(1):37–46, 1985.

(15) J. L. BARRETT AND A. H. JOHNSON. The role of control in attributing intentional agency to inanimate objects. *Journal of Cognition and Culture*, 3(3):208–217, 2003.

(16) R. F. BAUMEISTER, M. GAILLIOT, C. N. DEWALL, AND M. OATEN. Self-regulation and personality: How interventions increase regulatory success, and how depletion moderates the effects of traits on behavior. *Journal of Personality*, 74:1773–1801, 2006.

(17) R. F. BAUMEISTER AND E. J. MASICAMPO. Conscious thought is for facilitating social and cultural interactions: How mental simulations serve the animal-culture interface. *Psychological Review*, 117(3):945–971, 2010.

(18) R. F. BAUMEISTER, E. J. MASICAMPO, AND K. D. VOHS. Do conscious thoughts cause behavior? *Annual Review of Psychology*, 62:331–361, 2011.

(19) R. F. BAUMEISTER, B. J. SCHMEICHEL, C. N. DEWALL, AND K. D. VOHS. Is the conscious self a help, a hindrance, or an irrelevance to the creative process? *Advances in Psychology Research*, 53:137–152, 2006.

(20) R. F. BAUMEISTER, J. M. TWENGE, AND C. K. NUSS. Effects of social exclusion on cognitive processes: Anticipated aloneness reduces intelligent thought. *Journal of Personality and Social Psychology*, 83:817–827, 2002.

(21) R. F. BAUMEISTER, K. D. VOHS, AND D. M. TICE. The strength model of self-control. *Current Directions in Psychological Science*, 16:351–355, 2007.

(22) D. J. BEM. Self-perception: An alternative interpretation of cognitive dissonance phenomena. *Psychological Review*, 74(3):183–200, 1967.

(23) R. J. R. BLAIR. Responsiveness to distress cues in the child with psychopathic tendencies. *Personality and Individual Differences*, 27(1):135–145, 1999.

(24) R. J. R. BLAIR. The amygdala and ventromedial prefrontal cortex in morality and psychopathy. *Trends in Cognitive Sciences*, 11(9):387–392, 2007.

(25) L. B. BRÄCKER, K. P. SIJU, N. VARELA, Y. ASO, M. ZHANG, I. HEIN, M. L. VASCONCELOS, AND I. C. GRUNWALD KADOW. Essential role of the mushroom body in context-dependent $CO_2$ avoidance in *Drosophila*. *Current Biology*, 23(13):1228–1234, 2013.

(26) J. P. BRASIL-NETO, A. PASCUAL-LEONE, J. VALLS-SOLÉ, L. G. COHEN, AND M. HALLETT. Focal transcranial magnetic stimulation and response bias in a forced-choice task. *Journal of Neurology, Neurosurgery & Psychiatry*, 55(10):964–966, 1992.

(27) K. A. BRAUN, R. ELLIS, AND E. F. LOFTUS. Make my memory: How advertising can change our memories of the past. *Psychology & Marketing*, 19(1):1–23, 2002.

(28) C. A. BROWN, B. SEYMOUR, Y. BOYLE, W. EL-DEREDY, AND A. K. P. JONES. Modulation of pain ratings by expectation and uncertainty: Behavioral characteristics and anticipatory neural correlates. *Pain*, 135(3):240–250, 2008.

(29) J. M. BURGER. The foot-in-the-door compliance procedure: A multiple-process analysis and review. *Personality and Social Psychology Review*, 3(4):303–325, 1999.

(30) J. T. CACIOPPO, L. C. HAWKLEY, AND G. G. BERNSTON. The anatomy of loneliness. *Current Directions in Psychological Science*, 12:71–74, 2003.

(31) P. CARRUTHERS. How we know our own minds: The relationship between mindreading and metacognition. *Behavioral and Brain Sciences*, 32(2):121–182, 2009.

(32) H. A. CHAPMAN, D. A. KIM, J. M. SUSSKIND, AND A. K.

ANDERSON. In bad taste: Evidence for the oral origins of moral disgust. *Science*, 323:1222–1226, 2009.

(33) T. L. CHARTRAND AND J. A. BARGH. The chameleon effect: The perception-behavior link and social interaction. *Journal of Personality and Social Psychology*, 76:893–910, 1999.

(34) T. L. CHARTRAND, J. HUBER, B. SHIV, AND R. J. TANNER. Non-conscious goals and consumer choice. *Journal of Consumer Research*, 35(2):189–201, 2008.

(35) T. L. CHARTRAND, S. PINCKERT, AND J. M. BURGER. When manipulation backfires: The effects of time delay and requester on the foot-in-the-door technique. *Journal of Applied Social Psychology*, 29(1):211–221, 1999.

(36) M. CHEN AND J. A. BARGH. Nonconscious behavioral confirmation processes: The self-fulfilling consequences of automatic stereotype activation. *Journal of Experimental Social Psychology*, 33(5):541–560, 1997.

(37) J. J. CHRISTENSEN-SZALANSKI. Discount functions and the measurement of patients' values: Women's decisions during childbirth. *Medical Decision Making*, 4(1):47–58, 1984.

(38) R. B. CIALDINI. Crafting normative messages to protect the environment. *Current Directions in Psychological Science*, 12(4):105–109, 2003.

(39) R. B. CIALDINI, L. J. DEMAINE, B. J. SAGARIN, D. W. BARRETT, K. RHOADS, AND P. L. WINTER. Managing social norms for persuasive impact. *Social Influence*, 1(1):3–15, 2006.

(40) R. B. CIALDINI AND N. J. GOLDSTEIN. Social influence: Compliance and conformity. *Annual Review of Psychology*, 55:591–621, 2004.

(41) S. A. CLANCY, R. J. MCNALLY, D. L. SCHACTER, M. F. LENZENWEGER, AND R. K. PITMAN. Memory distortion in people reporting abduction by aliens. *Journal of Abnormal Psychology*, 111(3):455–461, 2002.

(42) J. J. CLARKSON, E. R. HIRT, L. JIA, AND M. B. ALEXANDER. When perception is more than reality: The effects of perceived versus actual resource depletion on self-regulatory behavior.

*Journal of Personality and Social Psychology*, 98(1):29–46, 2010.

(43) M. K. COLVIN AND M. S. GAZZANIGA. Split-brain cases. In M. S. VELMANS AND S. SCHNEIDER, editors, *The Blackwell Companion to Consciousness*, pages 181–193. Blackwell Publishing, 2006.

(44) J. CORRELL, B. PARK, C. M. JUDD, AND B. WITTENBRINK. The police officer's dilemma: Using ethnicity to disambiguate potentially threatening individuals. *Journal of Personality and Social Psychology*, 83(6):1314, 2002.

(45) R. CUSTERS AND H. AARTS. The unconscious will: How the pursuit of goals operates outside of conscious awareness. *Science*, 329(5987):47–50, 2010.

(46) J. M. DARLEY AND P. H. GROSS. A hypothesis-confirming bias in labeling effects. *Journal of Personality and Social Psychology*, 44(1):20–33, 1983.

(47) J. M. R. DELGADO. *Physical Control of the Mind: Toward a Psychocivilized Society*. Harper and Row, 1969.

(48) C. N. DEWALL, R. F. BAUMEISTER, AND E. J. MASICAMPO. Evidence that logical reasoning depends on conscious processing. *Consciousness and Cognition*, 17(3):628–645, 2008.

(49) A. DIJKSTERHUIS. Automaticity and the unconscious. In S. T. FISKE, D. T. GILBERT, AND G. LINDZEY, editors, *Handbook of Social Psychology*, pages 228–267, 2010.

(50) A. DIJKSTERHUIS, M. W. BOS, L. F. NORDGREN, AND R. B. VAN BAAREN. On making the right choice: The deliberation-without-attention effect. *Science*, 311(5763):1005–1007, 2006.

(51) J. DOYON AND H. BENALI. Reorganization and plasticity in the adult brain during learning of motor skills. *Current Opinion in Neurobiology*, 15(2):161–167, 2005.

(52) R. I. M. DUNBAR. The social brain hypothesis. *Evolutionary Anthropology*, 6:178–190, 1998.

(53) R. I. M. DUNBAR AND S. SHULTZ. Evolution in the social brain. *Science*, 317(5843):1344–1347, 2007.

(54) D. G. DUTTON AND A. P. ARON. Some evidence for heightened

sexual attraction under conditions of high anxiety. *Journal of Personality and Social Psychology*, 30:510–517, 1974.

(55) A. J. ELLIOT, D. NIESTA KAYER, T. GREITEMEYER, S. LICHTENFELD, R. H. GRAMZOW, M. A. MAIER, AND H. LIU. Red, rank, and romance in women viewing men. *Journal of Experimental Psychology: General*, 139:399–417, 2010.

(56) A. J. ELLIOT AND D. NIESTA. Romantic red: Red enhances men's attraction to women. *Journal of Personality and Social Psychology*, 95:1150–1164, 2008.

(57) N. EPLEY, A. WAYTZ, AND J. T. CACIOPPO. On seeing human: A three-factor theory of anthropomorphism. *Psychological Review*, 114(4):864–886, 2007.

(58) M. H. ERDELYI. A new look at the new look: Perceptual defense and vigilance. *Psychological Review*, 81(1):1–25, 1974.

(59) X. FANG, S. SINGH, AND R. AHLUWALIA. An examination of different explanations for the mere exposure effect. *Journal of Consumer Research*, 34(1):97–103, 2007.

(60) R. H. FAZIO, J. R. JACKSON, B. C. DUNTON, AND C. J. WILLIAMS. Variability in automatic activation as an unobtrusive measure of racial attitudes: A bona fide pipeline? *Journal of Personality and Social Psychology*, 69(6):1013–1027, 1995.

(61) R. FERRARO, J. R. BETTMAN, AND T. L. CHARTRAND. The power of strangers: The effect of incidental consumer brand encounters on brand choice. *Journal of Consumer Research*, 35(5):729–741, 2009.

(62) L. FESTINGER. *A Theory of Cognitive Dissonance*, 2. Stanford University Press, 1962.

(63) L. FESTINGER AND J. M. CARLSMITH. Cognitive consequences of forced compliance. *The Journal of Abnormal and Social Psychology*, 58(2):203–210, 1959.

(64) L. FESTINGER, H. W. RIECKEN, AND S. SCHACHTER. *When Prophecy Fails*. University of Minnesota Press, 1956.

(65) A. FLOYER-LEA AND P. M. MATTHEWS. Changing brain networks for visuomotor control with increased movement automaticity. *Journal of Neurophysiology*, 92(4):2405–2412, 2004.

(66) P. FOURNERET AND M. JEANNEROD. Limited conscious monitoring of motor performance in normal subjects. *Neuropsychologia*, 36(11):1133–1140, 1998.

(67) J. L. FREEDMAN AND S. C. FRASER. Compliance without pressure: The foot-in-the-door technique. *Journal of Personality and Social Psychology*, 4(2):195, 1966.

(68) U. FRITH AND F. HAPPÉ. Theory of mind and self-consciousness: What is it like to be autistic? *Mind and Language*, 14(1):82–89, 1999.

(69) M. T. GAILLIOT AND R. F. BAUMEISTER. The physiology of willpower. *Personality and Social Psychology Review*, 11(4):303–327, 2007.

(70) M. T. GAILLIOT AND R. F. BAUMEISTER. Self-regulation and sexual restraint: Dispositionally and temporarily poor self-regulatory abilities contribute to failures at restraining sexual behavior. *Personality and Social Psychology Bulletin*, 33(2):173–186, 2007.

(71) M. T. GAILLIOT, R. F. BAUMEISTER, C. N. DEWALL, J. K. MANER, E. A. PLANT, D. M. TICE, L. E. BREWER, AND B. J. SCHMEICHEL. Self-control relies on glucose as a limited energy source: Willpower is more than a metaphor. *Journal of Personality and Social Psychology*, 92:325–336, 2007.

(72) M. T. GAILLIOT, B. M. PERUCHE, E. A. PLANT, AND R. F. BAUMEISTER. Stereotypes and prejudice in the blood: Sucrose drinks reduce prejudice and stereotyping. *Journal of Experimental Social Psychology*, 45(1):288–290, 2009.

(73) M. S. GAZZANIGA. Cerebral specialization and interhemispheric communication: Does the corpus callosum enable the human condition? *Brain*, 123(7):1293–1326, 2000.

(74) N. J. GOLDSTEIN, R. B. CIALDINI, AND V. GRISKEVICIUS. A room with a viewpoint: Using social norms to motivate environmental conservation in hotels. *Journal of Consumer Research*, 35(3):472–482, 2008.

(75) J. D. GREENE, L. E. NYSTROM, A. D. ENGELL, J. M. DARLEY, AND J. D. COHEN. The neural bases of cognitive conflict and control in moral judgment. *Neuron*, 44(2):389–400, 2004.

(76) J. D. GREENE, R. B. SOMMERVILLE, L. E. NYSTROM, J. M. DARLEY, AND J. D. COHEN. An fMRI investigation of emotional engagement in moral judgment. *Science*, 293:2105–2108, 2001.

(77) A. G. GREENWALD, D. E. MCGHEE, AND J. L. K. SCHWARTZ. Measuring individual differences in implicit cognition: The implicit association test. *Journal of Personality and Social Psychology*, 74(6):1464–1480, 1998.

(78) D. M. GROMET AND E. PRONIN. What were you worried about? Actors' concerns about revealing fears and insecurities relative to observers' reactions. *Self and Identity*, 8(4):342–364, 2009.

(79) N. GUÉGUEN. Mimicry and seduction: An evaluation in a courtship context. *Social Influence*, 4:249–255, 2009.

(80) C. L. HAFER AND L. BÉGUE. Experimental research on just-world theory: Problems, developments, and future challenges. *Psychological Bulletin*, 131:128–167, 2005.

(81) A. M. HAFFENDEN, K. C. SCHIFF, AND M. A. GOODALE. The dissociation between perception and action in the Ebbinghaus illusion: Nonillusory effects of pictorial cues on grasp. *Current Biology*, 11(3):177–181, 2001.

(82) J. HAIDT AND S. KESEBIR. Morality. In S. T. FISKE, D. T. GILBERT, AND G. LINDZEY, editors, *Handbook of Social Psychology*, pages 797–832. 2010.

(83) W. T. HARBAUGH, U. MAYR, AND D. R. BURGHART. Neural responses to taxation and voluntary giving reveal motives for charitable donations. *Science*, 316:1622–1625, 2007.

(84) R. D. HARE, S. D. HART, AND T. J. HARPUR. Psychopathy and the DSM-IV criteria for antisocial personality disorder. *Journal of Abnormal Psychology*, 100(3):391–398, 1991.

(85) A. A. HARRISON. Mere exposure. *Advances in Experimental Social Psychology*, 10:39–83, 1977.

(86) L. C. HAWKLEY AND J. T. CACIOPPO. Loneliness and pathways to disease. *Brain, Behavior, and Immunity*, 17:S98–S105, 2002.

(87) M. HÖFLE, M. HAUCK, A. K. ENGEL, AND D. SENKOWSKI. Viewing a needle pricking a hand that you perceive as yours enhances unpleasantness of pain. *Pain*, 153(5):1074–1081, 2012.

(88) D. HUME. *Enquiries concerning Human Understanding and concerning the Principles of Morals.* Oxford University Press, 1777.

(89) N. HUMPHREY. *The Inner Eye.* Faber, 1986.

(90) N. HUMPHREY. *Soul Dust.* Princeton University Press, 2011.

(91) M. INZLICHT AND B. J. SCHMEICHEL. What is ego depletion? Toward a mechanistic revision of the resource model of self-control. *Perspectives on Psychological Science,* 7(5):450–463, 2012.

(92) M. JEANNEROD. Consciousness of action as an embodied consciousness. In S. POCKETT, W. P. BANKS, AND S. GALLAGHER, editors, *Does Consciousness Cause Behavior,* pages 25–38. MIT Press, 2006.

(93) V. JOB, C. S. DWECK, AND G. M. WALTON. Ego depletion – is it all in your head? Implicit theories about willpower affect self-regulation. *Psychological Science,* 21(11):1686–1693, 2010.

(94) P. JOHANSSON, L. HALL, S. SIKSTROM, AND A. OLSSON. Failure to detect mismatches between intention and outcome in a simple decision task. *Science,* 310:116–119, 2005.

(95) R. KAUFMAN. *Inside Scientology.* The Olympia Press, 1972.

(96) J. KNOBE. Intentional action and side effects in ordinary language. *Analysis,* 63(279):190–194, 2003.

(97) M. KOENIGS, L. YOUNG, R. ADOLPHS, D. TRANEL, F. CUSHMAN, M. HAUSER, AND A. DAMASIO. Damage to the prefrontal cortex increases utilitarian moral judgements. *Nature,* 446(7138):908–911, 2007.

(98) T. KOGUT AND I. RITOV. The 'identified victim' effect: An identified group, or just a single individual? *Journal of Behavioral Decision Making,* 18(3):157–167, 2005.

(99) M. KOSFELD, M. HEINRICHS, P. J. ZAK, U. FISCHBACHER, AND E. FEHR. Oxytocin increases trust in humans. *Nature,* 435(7042):673–676, 2005.

(100) A. W. KRUGLANSKI, S. ALON, AND T. LEWIS. Retrospective misattribution and task enjoyment. *Journal of Experimental Social Psychology,* 8(6):493–501, 1972.

(101) W. R. KUNST-WILSON AND R. B. ZAJONC. Affective

discrimination of stimuli that cannot be recognized. *Science*, 207:557–558, 1980.

(102) J. L. LAKIN, V. E. JEFFERIS, C. M. CHENG, AND T. L. CHARTRAND. The chameleon effect as social glue: Evidence for the evolutionary significance of nonconscious mimicry. *Journal of Non-Verbal Behavior*, 27(3):145–162, 2003.

(103) G. LAKOFF AND M. JOHNSON. *Metaphors We Live By*. University of Chicago Press, 1981.

(104) M. J. LERNER. Observer's evaluation of a victim: Justice, guilt, and veridical perception. *Journal of Personality and Social Psychology*, 20:127–135, 1971.

(105) M. J. LERNER AND C. H. SIMMONS. Observer's reaction to the 'innocent victim': Compassion or rejection? *Journal of Personality and Social Psychology*, 4(2):203–210, 1966.

(106) P. LEWICKI, T. HILL, AND E. BIZOT. Acquisition of procedural knowledge about a pattern of stimuli that cannot be articulated. *Cognitive Psychology*, 20(1):24–37, 1988.

(107) B. LIBET. Unconscious cerebral initiative and the role of conscious will in voluntary action. 8:529–566, 1985.

(108) E. F. LOFTUS AND J. C. PALMER. Reconstruction of automobile destruction: An example of the interaction between language and memory. *Journal of Verbal Learning and Verbal Behavior*, 13(5):585–589, 1974.

(109) E. F. LOFTUS AND J. E. PICKRELL. The formation of false memories. *Psychiatric Annals*, 25(12):720–725, 1995.

(110) G. D. LOGAN AND M. J. C. CRUMP. Cognitive illusions of authorship reveal hierarchical error detection in skilled typists. *Science*, 330(6004):683–686, 2010.

(111) C. G. LORD, L. ROSS, AND M. R. LEPPER. Biased assimilation and attitude polarization: The effects of prior theories on subsequently considered evidence. *Journal of Personality and Social Psychology*, 37:2098–2109, 1979.

(112) N. R. F. MAIER. Reasoning in humans. ii. The solution of a problem and its appearance in consciousness. *Journal of Comparative Psychology*, 12(2):181, 1931.

(113) M. MCCLOSKEY AND M. ZARAGOZA. Misleading postevent information and memory for events: Arguments and evidence against memory impairment hypotheses. *Journal of Experimental Psychology: General*, 114(1):1–16, 1985.

(114) E. MCGINNIES. Emotionality and perceptual defense. *Psychological Review*, 56(5):244–251, 1949.

(115) H. MCGURK AND J. MACDONALD. Hearing lips and seeing voices. *Nature*, 1976.

(116) N. L. MEAD, R. F. BAUMEISTER, F. GINO, M. E. SCHWEITZER, AND D. ARIELY. Too tired to tell the truth: Self-control resource depletion and dishonesty. *Journal of Experimental Social Psychology*, 45(3):594–597, 2009.

(117) B. E. MEYEROWITZ, J. G. WILLIAMS, AND J. GESSNER. Perceptions of controllability and attitudes toward cancer and cancer patients. *Journal of Applied Social Psychology*, 17:471–492, 1987.

(118) D. C. MOLDEN, C. M. HUI, A. A. SCHOLER, B. P. MEIER, E. E. NOREEN, P. R. DAGOSTINO, AND V. MARTIN. Motivational versus metabolic effects of carbohydrates on self-control. *Psychological Science*, 23(10):1137–1144, 2012.

(119) N. MORAY. Attention in dichotic listening: Affective cues and the influence of instructions. *Quarterly Journal of Experimental Psychology*, 11(1):56–60, 1959.

(120) E. MORSELLA. The function of phenomenal states: Supramodular interaction theory. *Psychological Review*, 112(4): 1000–1021, 2005.

(121) E. MORSELLA AND J. A. BARGH. Unconscious action tendencies: Sources of 'un-integrated' action. In DECETY AND CACIOPPO, editors, *Handbook of Social Neuroscience*. 2011.

(122) E. MORSELLA, S. C. KRIEGER, AND J. A. BARGH. The primary function of consciousness: Why skeletal muscles are voluntary muscles. In E. MORSELLA, J. A. BARGH, AND P. M. GOLLWITZER, editors, *Oxford Handbook of Human Action*, pages 625–634. 2009.

(123) M. MURAVEN AND R. F. BAUMEISTER. Self-regulation and

depletion of limited resources: Does self-control resemble a muscle? *Psychological Bulletin*, 126(2):247–259, 2000.

(124) M. MURAVEN, D. M. TICE, AND R. F. BAUMEISTER. Self-control as a limited resource: Regulatory depletion patterns. *Journal of Personality and Social Psychology*, 74:774–789, 1998.

(125) R. E. NISBETT AND T. D. WILSON. Telling more than we can know: Verbal reports on mental processes. *Psychological Review*, 84(3):231–259, 1977.

(126) B. A. NOSEK, A. G. GREENWALD, AND M. R. BANAJI. The implicit association test at age 7: A methodological and conceptual review. In J. A. BARGH, editor, *Social Psychology and the Unconscious: The Automaticity of Higher Mental Processes*, pages 265–292. 2007.

(127) M. OATEN AND K. CHENG. Longitudinal gains in self-regulation from regular physical exercise. *British Journal of Health Psychology*, 11(4):717–733, 2006.

(128) B. K. PAYNE. Prejudice and perception: The role of automatic and controlled processes in misperceiving a weapon. *Journal of Personality and Social Psychology*, 81(2):181, 2001.

(129) R. M. PERLOFF. *The Dynamics of Persuasion*. Lawrence Erlbaum Associates, 2003.

(130) J. PERNER, U. FRITH, A. M. LESLIE, AND S. R. LEEKAM. Exploration of the autistic child's theory of mind: Knowledge, belief, and communication. *Child Development*, pages 689–700, 1989.

(131) M. PESSIGLIONE, L. SCHMIDT, B. DRAGANSKI, R. KALISCH, H. LAU, R. J. DOLAN, AND C. D. FRITH. How the brain translates money into force: A neuroimaging study of subliminal motivation. *Science*, 316(5826):904–906, 2007.

(132) W. PHILLIPS, S. BARON-COHEN, AND M. RUTTER. Understanding intention in normal development and in autism. *British Journal of Developmental Psychology*, 16(3):337–348, 1998.

(133) D. A. PIZARRO, C. LANEY, E. K. MORRIS, AND E. F. LOFTUS. Ripple effects in memory: Judgments of moral blame can distort memory for events. *Memory & Cognition*, 34(3):550–555, 2006.

(134) A. R. PRATKANIS. *The Science of Social Influence*. Psychology Press, 2007.

(135) E. PRONIN, C. Y. OLIVOLA, AND K. A. KENNEDY. Doing unto future selves as you would do unto others: Psychological distance and decision making. *Personality and Social Psychology Bulletin*, 34(2):224–236, 2008.

(136) D. READ AND B. VAN LEEUWEN. Predicting hunger: The effects of appetite and delay on choice. *Organizational Behavior and Human Decision Processes*, 76(2):189–205, 1998.

(137) A. S. REBER. Implicit learning of artificial grammars. *Journal of Verbal Learning and Verbal Behavior*, 6(6):855–863, 1967.

(138) A. S. REBER. Implicit learning and tacit knowledge. *Journal of Experimental Psychology: General*, 118(3):219–235, 1989.

(139) P. ROZIN, J. HAIDT, AND K. FINCHER. From oral to moral. *Science*, 323:1179–1180, 2009.

(140) K. SEKIYAMA AND Y. TOHKURA. McGurk effect in non-English listeners: Few visual effects for Japanese subjects hearing Japanese syllables of high auditory intelligibility. *The Journal of the Acoustical Society of America*, 90:1797–1805, 1991.

(141) L. SHAMS, Y. KAMITANI, AND S. SHIMOJO. What you see is what you hear. *Nature*, 408:788, 2000.

(142) L. SHAMS, Y. KAMITANI, AND S. SHIMOJO. Visual illusion induced by sound. *Cognitive Brain Research*, 14(1):147–152, 2002.

(143) Y. SHODA, W. MISCHEL, AND P. K. PEAKE. Predicting adolescent cognitive and self-regulatory competencies from preschool delay of gratification: Identifying diagnostic conditions. *Developmental Psychology*, 26(6):978–986, 1990.

(144) T. SINGER, B. SEYMOUR, J. P. O'DOHERTY, K. E. STEPHAN, R. J. DOLAN, AND C. D. FRITH. Empathic neural responses are modulated by the perceived fairness of others. *Nature*, 439:466–469, 2006.

(145) A. SLACHEVSKY, B. PILLON, P. FOURNERET, P. PRADAT-DIEHL, M. JEANNEROD, AND B. DUBOIS. Preserved adjustment but impaired awareness in a sensory-motor conflict following pre-frontal lesions. *Journal of Cognitive Neuroscience*, 13(3):332–340, 2001.

(146) D. A. SMALL, G. LOEWENSTEIN, AND P. SLOVIC. Sympathy and callousness: The impact of deliberative thought on donations to identifiable and statistical victims. *Organizational Behavior and Human Decision Processes*, 102(2):143–153, 2007.

(147) A. P. SMITH, R. CLARK, AND J. GALLAGHER. Breakfast cereal and caffeinated coffee: Effects on working memory, attention, mood, and cardiovascular function. *Physiology & Behavior*, 67(1):9–17, 1999.

(148) VICTORIA SOUTHGATE. Early manifestations of mindreading. In S. BARON-COHEN, H. TAGER-FLUSBERG, AND M. V. LOMBARDO, editors, *Understanding Other Minds*, pages 3–18. Oxford University Press, 2013.

(149) S. STEPPER AND F. STRACK. Proprioceptive determinants of emotional and nonemotional feelings. *Journal of Personality and Social Psychology*, 64:211–220, 1993.

(150) T. F. STILLMAN, D. M. TICE, F. D. FINCHAM, AND N. M. LAMBERT. The psychological presence of family improves self-control. *Journal of Social and Clinical Psychology*, 28(4):498–529, 2009.

(151) J. P. TANGNEY, R. F. BAUMEISTER, AND A. L. BOONE. High self-control predicts good adjustment, less pathology, better grades, and interpersonal success. *Journal of Personality*, 72(2):271–324, 2004.

(152) A. TODOROV, A. N. MANDISODZA, A. GOREN, AND C. C. HALL. Inferences of competence from faces predict election outcomes. *Science*, 308(5728):1623–1626, 2005.

(153) J. M. TWENGE, R. F. BAUMEISTER, C. NATHAN DEWALL, N. CIAROCCO, AND J. MICHAEL BARTELS. Social exclusion decreases prosocial behavior. *Journal of Personality and Social Psychology*, 92:56–66, 2007.

(154) J. M. TWENGE, R. F. BAUMEISTER, D. M. TICE, AND T. S. STUCKE. If you can't join them, beat them: Effects of social exclusion on aggressive behavior. *Journal of Personality and Social Psychology*, 81:1058–1069, 2001.

(155) J. M. TWENGE, L. ZHANG, AND C. IM. It's beyond my control: A cross-temporal meta-analysis of increasing externality

in locus of control, 1960-2002. *Personality and Social Psychology Review*, 8(3):308–319, 2004.

(156) E. L. UHLMANN, D. A. PIZARRO, D. TANNENBAUM, AND P. H. DITTO. The motivated use of moral principles. *Judgment and Decision Making*, 4(6):476–491, 2009.

(157) R. B. VAN BAAREN, R. W. HOLLAND, B. STEENAERT, AND A. VAN KNIPPENBERG. Mimicry for money: Behavioral consequences of imitation. *Journal of Experimental Social Psychology*, 39:393–398, 2003.

(158) L. VAN BOVEN, G. LOEWENSTEIN, AND D. DUNNING. The illusion of courage in social predictions: Underestimating the impact of fear of embarrassment on other people. *Organizational Behavior and Human Decision Processes*, 96(2):130–141, 2005.

(159) L. VAN BOVEN, G. LOEWENSTEIN, E. WELCH, AND D. DUNNING. The illusion of courage in self-predictions: Mispredicting one's own behavior in embarrassing situations. *Journal of Behavioral Decision Making*, 25(1):1–12, 2012.

(160) M. VELMANS AND S. SCHNEIDER. *The Blackwell Companion to Consciousness*. Blackwell, 2007.

(161) M. VIRKUNNEN, J. DE JONG, J. BARTKO and F. K. GOODWIN AND M. LINNOILA. *Relationship of psychobiological variables to recidivism in violent offenders and impulsive fire setters: a follow-up study*. Archives of General Psychiatry, 46(7):600, 1989.

(162) K. D. VOHS, R. F. BAUMEISTER, B. J. SCHMEICHEL, J. M. TWENGE, N. M. NELSON, AND D. M. TICE. Making choices impairs subsequent self-control: A limited-resource account of decision-making, self-regulation, and active initiative. *Journal of Personality and Social Psychology*, 94(5):883–898, 2008.

(163) K. D. VOHS AND J. W. SCHOOLER. The value of believing in free will: Encouraging a belief in determinism increases cheating. *Psychological Science*, 19(1):49–54, 2008.

(164) K. A. WADE, M. GARRY, J. D. READ, AND D. S. LINDSAY. A picture is worth a thousand lies: Using false photographs to create false childhood memories. *Psychonomic Bulletin & Review*, 9(3):597–603, 2002.

(165) D. M. WEGNER. *The Illusion of Conscious Will*. MIT Press, 2002.

(166) L. WEISKRANTZ. *Blindsight*. Oxford University Press, 2009.

(167) G. L. WELLS AND R. E. PETTY. The effects of over head movements on persuasion: Compatibility and incompatibility of responses. *Basic and Applied Social Psychology*, 1(3):219–230, 1980.

(168) R. WEST. Glucose for smoking cessation. *CNS Drugs*, 15(4):261–265, 2001.

(169) J. WHITHAM AND A. MATHIS. Effects of hunger and predation risk on foraging behavior of graybelly salamanders, *Eurycea Multiplicata*. *Journal of Chemical Ecology*, 26(7):1659–1665, 2000.

(170) L. E. WILLAMS AND J. A. BARGH. Experiencing physical warmth promotes interpersonal warmth. *Science*, 322:606–607, 2008.

(171) D. WILLIAMS. Theory of own mind in autism: Evidence of a specific deficit in self-awareness? *Autism*, 14(5):474–494, 2010.

(172) T. D. WILSON, D. J. LISLE, J. W. SCHOOLER, S. D. HODGES, K. J. KLAAREN, AND S. J. LAFLEUR. Introspecting about reasons can reduce post-choice satisfaction. *Personality and Social Psychology Bulletin*, 19:331–339, 1993.

(173) J. C. WU, J. C. GILLIN, M. S. BUCHSBAUM, AND T. HERSHEY. The effect of sleep deprivation on cerebral glucose metabolic rate in normal humans assessed with positron emission tomography. *Sleep: Journal of Sleep Research & Sleep Medicine*, 14(2):155–162, 1991.

(174) R. B. ZAJONC. Attitudinal effects of mere exposure. *Journal of Personality and Social Psychology*, 9(2):1–27, 1968.

(175) R. ZIEGLER AND M. DIEHL. Is politician A or politician B more persuasive? *European Journal of Social Psychology*, 33:623–627, 2003.

(176) C. ZHONG AND G. J. LEONARDELLI. Cold and lonely: Does social exclusion literally feel cold? *Psychological Science*, 19:838–842, 2008.

(177) C. ZHONG AND K. LILJENQUIST. Washing away your sins: Threatened morality and physical cleansing. *Science*, 313:1451–1452, 2006.

In the best books, the ending often comes as a shock.
Not just because of that one last twist in the tale,
but because you have been so absorbed in their world,
that coming back to the harsh light of reality is a jolt.

If that describes you now, then perhaps you should track down
some new leads, and find new suspense in other worlds.

Join us at www.hodder.co.uk, or follow us on
Twitter @hodderbooks, and you can tap in to a
community of fellow thrill-seekers.

Whether you want to find out more about this book,
or a particular author, watch trailers and interviews, have
the chance to win early limited editions, or simply browse
our expert readers' selection of the very best books,
we think you'll find what you're looking for.

And if you don't, that's the place to tell us what's missing.

**We love what we do, and we'd love you to be part of it.**

www.hodder.co.uk

 @hodderbooks

HodderBooks

HodderBooks